DOG TRAINING
FOR THE
PHYSICALLY CHALLENGED

By Ilsa M. Sternberg
Illustrated By Margaret S. Pape

Circustoo

P.O. BOX 578, North White Plains, NY 10603

DOG TRAINING FOR THE PHYSICALLY CHALLENGED

By Ilsa M. Sternberg

Illustrated By Margaret S. Pape

Published by: Circustoo
P.O.Box 578
North White Plains, NY 10603

ISBN 0-9660435-0-2

First Printing, 1997

Printed in the United States of America

This book is lovingly dedicated to my dad, Henry, who gave me his support and the encouragement to achieve my goals.

In recognition of my past partners;

Calbak Dark Cloud of Bo-Jib, CDX, TD, WC, Can CD
Wildwood Kine-ahora Shayner, UDT, WC, Can CDX
CH Rushcreek Kine-ahora Ketzel, TD
CH Arbeitsheim's Choice Chablis, UDT, Can CD, PCA
    DOM
CH Stouravon Burghbridge Princess Suki, UDT, Can
    CD
CH Debonair Copyright, UDT
AM/Can CH. Kine-ahora Debonair Pilot, Am/Can CD
CH Kine-ahora Joy, UD, PCA DOM
CH Kine-ahora Almond Joy, UD
CH Kine-ahora Presto Change-O, CD, OA

Acknowledgments

I want to thank my long time personal aide and friend, Gwendolyn McCalla, for her assistance in the care of the numerous creatures who have entered our lives.

I am grateful to Lynn Chamberlain for her tireless navigation of several hundred thousand miles in pursuit of all those Championship points and qualifying scores.

I thank the breeder of my first Papillon, Carolyn Wells, for introducing me to the breed and encouraging my endeavors.

The following is a list of people who helped make this book a reality:

Margaret Shafer Pape

Richard Pape

Deborah Lee, *Three Dog's Running Studio for Animals Only*

Rick Hayden

Deborah Paruolo

Gerrianne Darnell

Ken Berenson

Joseph F. Joly

Robert Hughes

Kenneth Di Lorenzo

M. Christine Zink, D.V.M., Ph.D.

Jeannette Ringer

Katie Souder

PREFACE

I have been asked to write this book by dog trainers who receive requests from physically disabled dog owners wishing to train their dogs either for obedience competition or simply to have a well behaved companion.

There is a growing number of physically disabled people who wish to get into the sport of showing dogs or people who realize the value of a well trained dog that is able to assist in their daily life. A dog - able to retrieve or carry any object or one that will speak on command to call for help - is a definite asset to a disabled person. A well trained dog helps bridge the gap between a child and a person who sits in a wheelchair or has other physical impairments. The child relates to the dog and then relates to the person.

I have trained my own Golden Retrievers, Chesapeake Bay Retriever and Papillons to 6 UD's and 6 TD's, 2 working certificates and many breed championships. In addition to my own dogs, I have assisted in the training of many other breeds including Huskies, Brittanys, Springers, Vizslas, Salukis, a Schnauzer and a Poodle.

Most of the training techniques used in this book are applicable to "able bodied" trainers, and these techniques are a composite of methods I have studied over the past 25 years plus my own personal experiences. Besides the number of physically challenged dog trainers that might find this book useful, I'm certain that there are quite a number of lazy folk out there who might enjoy a "sit in a chair and train your dog" method.

I owe a deep debt of gratitude to the late William Koehler who shaped my conception of a well-trained dog and who spent the time showing me how to successfully achieve the desired results from a wheelchair. I recommend reading all of Bill Koehler's books on dog training.

I want to thank my friend, Jacquelin Werb and the late CH Josandre's Katydid Cadenza UD, Can CDX, Ber CD for inspiring me with their display of teamwork in the obedience ring. They were the first dog and handler team I met who presented the picture of a team that truly enjoyed working together. I think that whatever training method you use, the end result should be a dog that thoroughly enjoys working for her handler and a handler that appreciates her dog's efforts.

A properly motivated dog enjoys a working relationship with her owner; the bond that training creates is a wonder to behold.

I hope this book helps you and your dog to develop the kind of relationship that I have enjoyed over the years with my own dogs.

TABLE OF CONTENTS

Chapter One

CHOOSING A BREED

Yeeeeeeeeeeeeha!

If you already have the dog you wish to train, I hope it is the right dog for you. Yet, so many people choose dogs that are not suitable for their disabilities or needs. For example, if you have very limited upper arm strength, a Malamute is not for you. If you need a dog to carry packages or to pull your chair, I would not recommend a Pekingese. You should study the jobs that different breeds were originally bred to perform. Some breeds are easily trained to work for humans, such as many varieties of Retrievers, some of the herding breeds, Dobes, etc. Terriers, hounds and some of the Northern breeds can be a bit self-involved, choosing to follow their own pleasures instead of pleasing their owner. Finding ways to motivate some of these breeds to be completely reliable can be a real challenge and quite time-consuming. Terriers can be quite willful, stubborn and may sometimes be aggressive toward other dogs. They also require grooming such as stripping or clipping, which might be a problem for someone with physical limitations. Hounds can be quite sensitive and may not accept food as a motivator when stressed, or may shut down with a heavy correction. You have to be a pretty experienced trainer to get a hound to enjoy working for you. The Northern breeds such as Huskies, Samoyeds, and Malamutes can have a strong desire to run. They are quite independent, and off lead control can be a problem

Of course there are exceptions in every breed, both positive and negative. For the novice trainer, it is worth the time to study the individual characteristics of the breeds, evaluate how much time and physical effort you can devote to training, and then make a selection with these two criteria in mind.

If the potential handler is a child, you might make the decision yourself as to the choice of a suitable breed. Allow the child to pick the puppy in the litter to which he most relates.

If you are not interested in competing at AKC sanctioned events, you might consider saving the life of a mixed breed from a shelter. Older dogs are readily available and you can easily evaluate the dog's established temperament, size and maintenance.

Sometimes breeders have older dogs available that are retired from the show ring or from breeding. These dogs can make wonderful pets if they have received the proper socialization and training from their breeders. You can avoid dealing with naughty puppy habits this way. Many of these dogs are housebroken, over the teething stage, leash and crate trained, and ready to go to a home where they will get individual love and attention. Older dogs readily form strong attachments to their new owner. I have personally placed a number of older dogs. While I find placing a dog I've lived with to be quite difficult for me, after a short period of adjustment the dog and his new owner form a bond that is truly incredible. When the dog comes back for a visit she is happy to see me and the other dogs, but she can't wait to return home with her adoptive folks. Matching dogs and owners in a permanent, loving relationship is my greatest joy as a breeder and overrides the heartaches of breeding that you often encounter.

A final word on the subject. If you already have a dog that is proving difficult to train, you can hire a trainer to help you. However, the trainer must be willing to work with you and the dog, and he or she must be willing to compromise their training techniques to fit the situation. I use food only as a tool to initially motivate the dog to work for me. The end result should be a dog that above all else, with all of her heart, wishes to obey the commands of her handler. A dog can fail a recall in the obedience ring at the cost of a qualifying ribbon. In the real world, ignoring a recall can cost the dog her life.

Chapter Two

PHILOSOPHY

Over the years, I have gathered training techniques from observing other trainers and attending countless seminars. I believe that studying the behavior patterns and understanding the nature of the breed of dog with whom you are working is beneficial to the training of the animal. I learn a great deal about my dogs by simply watching them playing in the yard and interacting with each other. I can tell which dogs are dominant, how much correction they will accept from one another, which dogs seek out the shade and which dogs enjoy playing hard in the sun. All of these factors determine what I can accept from them during a training session. When buying a new car, you must understand the basic options before you can drive it. Just as you spend time reading the owner's manual and getting to know your car, you must also get to know and understand your dog. Unfortunately, there are too many failed human/dog relationships and these failures can lead to serious consequences such as dog bites, abusively trained dogs or a complete failure in the relationship which can result in the death of the dog.

When I encounter a "bad training day," and believe me there are more than a few of those, I ask, what is wrong with this picture? Why am I not able to communicate with this dog today? Why can I not teach this particular exercise to this particular dog, when I've successfully taught it to other dogs in the past? If I stop what I am doing and I take the time to reflect on the problem, I can usually work it out - usually at 2 AM while the rest of the sane world is sleeping!

Perhaps my current dog has a phobia about being touched in a particular spot or she has a fear of the place I'm training at that day. Perhaps another dog being trained in the class is aggressive, acting up or intimidating my dog. I must then concentrate on putting my dog at ease with the situation. You can not teach a dog a new behavior or exercise when she is experiencing fear or is in a hostile or distracting environment.

On the other hand, perhaps I am the one with the problem. Due to my disability, my arms may not be as capable of making the corrections as they were five years ago. I then have to either figure out another way, or I ask for some physical assistance. It could be that I'm tired today, or maybe I'm rushing the training session, or I'm pushing the dog too fast. In dealing with physical disabilities, you must consider how you can get the dog to respond with regard to the capability of the individual. My muscular weakness impairs the volume of my voice and decreases my respiration. Sometimes my voice is barely above a whisper. This can pose a definite problem in a noisy, crowded arena. While other handlers can compensate for their dog's inattention by giving loud, decisive commands, my dogs have to be especially attuned to my changing physical conditions.

I believe in treating a dog fairly and honestly. I use food to develop a training relationship with my dog, to bring her up close to me and to direct her attention to my hands, while teaching her to respond to my soft voice. But I also use some amount of force, because a dog is by nature a pack animal who responds to and respects its pack leader. Being a small person without a great deal of physical strength, I must ensure, without question, that I am the leader of my dog's pack. Contention over who is pack leader may arise when I am trimming nails, whiskers or feet or when teaching the retrieve, but a dog that does not respect me, or considers herself dominant over me, leaves my house forever. If a dog has this problem only with me, I find her another home. If a dog has a dominance problem with everyone, I consider her a danger to society. There are plenty of wonderful dogs in this world that are deserving of a good home.

I usually use a prong collar on all breeds beginning at twelve weeks for a toy dog and seven weeks for a medium to large dog. I use it with a buckle or choke collar so the dog gets used to wearing both collars. I can usually dispense with the prong by the time she reaches eighteen months. I have successfully used a prong collar on all of my young dogs. Because of my limited arm strength I am unable to stop a dog from pulling on a lead or from sniffing the ground using other types of collars. The prong collar discourages the dog from forming these undesired habits when used correctly. I don't give violent jerks on the prong collar. Instead I maintain a constant tension on the lead and the collar self-corrects the dog. If the dog continues to pull or sniff the ground, I am then able to give mild collar corrections within my physical capability. Choke collars direct the force of the correction to one place on the neck which can cause tracheal damage to the dog. I do not have enough strength to effect a correction on a buckle collar. It is important to teach the dog to walk on a loose lead without pulling or sniffing the ground. This is one of the keys to getting the dog to eventually heel off lead. Once the dog has developed a sensitivity to mild collar corrections on the prong collar, I am able to transfer to a choke or buckle collar.

I use a heavy lead to teach all exercises and then transfer to a lightweight lead to make the transition to off lead work. Please note: I NEVER attempt off lead work until the dog is consistently performing satisfactorily on a light, loose lead attached to a buckle or choke collar. A physically-limited person *MUST* have a RELIABLE dog, because he or she can't grab or run down a dog that is out of reach, running away or out of control.

I use an ear pinch or a collar twist for the retrieve depending upon the temperament of the dog and the ability of the handler.

These methods are necessary to ensure the total reliability that a physically disabled person must have in her dog. These techniques are those I have used successfully on my own dogs. This book is merely an aid to assist people with physical limitations in training their own dogs. If you are successful in finding other methods, please pass them on to me. I always keep an open mind.

My first obedience seminar was instructed by Bill Koehler. Prior to that seminar I was working my Chesapeake Bay Retriever, "Cloudy," who had been trained in Novice obedience and retrieving by her breeder. I muddled through Cloudy's CDX and was attempting Utility when I acquired a Golden Retriever puppy named "Chico." At three months of age I took Chico to Koehler's seminar. After listening to the first hour of the seminar I realized I had discovered the only trainer who had techniques applicable to my situation. I began to ask questions and within a short time Mr. Koehler was primarily directing the seminar towards me. He realized my immediate need to gain control of a puppy who was going to grow into a large, unmanageable dog. Mr. Koehler even gave up his lunch breaks to work with me and my puppy. His technique with the longe line to get reliable off lead heeling was my first realization that I could actually train a dog by myself. He showed me that with proper use of a prong collar and light line I could use a minimum of physical ability to control a potentially large, strong dog. Mr. Koehler's philosophy of achieving absolute control under distracting situations using a minimum of physical effort was one to which I could relate. I left that seminar with the tools and knowledge of how to achieve an obedience trained dog. When Chico and I earned our 3rd Utility leg about 3 ½ years later I wrote to Bill thanking him for his efforts on my behalf. I wanted him to know his contribution to my success in dog training. After training six of my own Utility Dogs, Bill Koehler's training techniques still form the foundation for my training.

Chapter Three

BONDING

Bonding with your dog is critical. In my house someone else feeds my dogs, lets them out of their crates, and bathes them. But oddly enough my dogs relate and respond better to me than to the person who essentially cares for them. I believe it is because of the quality time I spend bonding with each dog.

Food is a great way to bond with a dog. I microwave hot dogs and I keep them in a pouch attached with Velcro to my wheelchair. One quarter of a hot dog lasts about a 15 minute bonding session for a small dog. Very tiny pieces are used. I would double the amount of food, to a half of a hot dog, for a large dog. I slice the hot dog in half and then slice the half lengthwise. If you have the time, you can get a lot of training accomplished by working a few minutes at a time, several times a day. Your dog will respond better to you if she is kept confined in a crate for at least a half an hour before your training session.

If you are working with a large dog that you can easily reach, put the dog on lead, call it to you by name and give it a tiny treat. While the dog is receiving the treat you stroke the dog on the head, around the muzzle, eyes, ears, etc. Make sure the dog is as close to you as possible by enticing her to rest her head on your lap. When the dog is comfortable with this, you can begin to examine her head, lifting the lips, running a finger over the teeth, examining ears, and opening the mouth. Give treats to the dog, speak softly, and stroke the places you are touching. If the dog objects to being examined, hold her firmly and give an emphatic "no" while continuing the examination. You must take the attitude that since you are providing food, shelter, medical care and affection for this dog, you are entitled to access all parts of her body. This is a step toward establishing dominance as well as facilitating grooming and training.

When the dog looks forward to this physical contact, you can continue stroking her head with your hands while touching her legs and belly with your feet. If you are unable to use your feet, you can use a 3' long 3/8" wide dowel to stroke the dog, moving it slowly along the dog's body while feeding her pieces of hot dogs and speaking in a soothing tone. Not only is the dog deriving pleasure from the stroking, but you are establishing the ground work for a variety of exercises such as the retrieve, the stand for exam, the down, and the recall, as well as being able to clean ears, teeth and administer oral medications.

If you are working with a small to medium-sized dog, you must teach the dog to jump up on a chair, couch, bed, bench or stool so you can reach her. Put the dog on lead and induce the dog to jump up on a low, flat bench or chair by tossing a piece of hot dog just out of her reach. When the dog jumps up on the bench, praise her while she eats the food. Feed her another piece while she is up there. Have her jump down and continue to repeat the behavior until she is readily jumping on and off on the command "get up". The next step is teaching the dog to come close and putting her feet on your lap. Use food to encourage this. Use a voice command and pat your lap. The dog must understand that putting her feet on your lap, or the next step which is jumping into your lap, is by invitation only. After all, you may not want a wet, muddy dog on your lap, but you do want to be able to call her up when needed. When you want the behavior, encourage it with a command, food and praise. Discourage it at all other times. Believe me, your dog will learn the difference.

I teach down, stand, stay, retrieving and grooming manners on a grooming table. If that is not convenient, you may use a chair, couch, bed or anything that is accessible for you. Once the dog is readily jumping up on a chair and then onto your lap, training the dog to jump from lap to table can begin.

Before bringing the dog to the table, place a small piece of hot dog on the far side of the table. The dog will not see you place it, and she will always think food will somehow appear on the table. Get the dog on your lap, and bring her over to the table. Chances are she will sniff out the food and try to reach it.

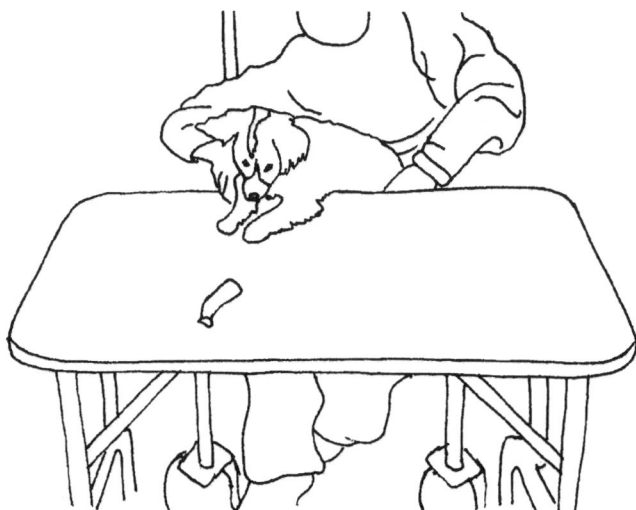

Hopefully, the only way she can reach it is by jumping up on the table. If she doesn't see the food, take a small piece out of your pouch, let her sniff it and toss it on the table close to the other piece. Place your hands behind the dog's elbows while she is facing the table and gently push her up giving the command "up on the table." When she jumps up, allow her to eat both pieces of food. If you are unable to get her up yourself, have a helper stand on the far side of the table and pull the dog up to the food while *you give the commands and deliver the praise.* In all training exercises where you require assistance, make sure _you_ always issue the commands, praise and food rewards.

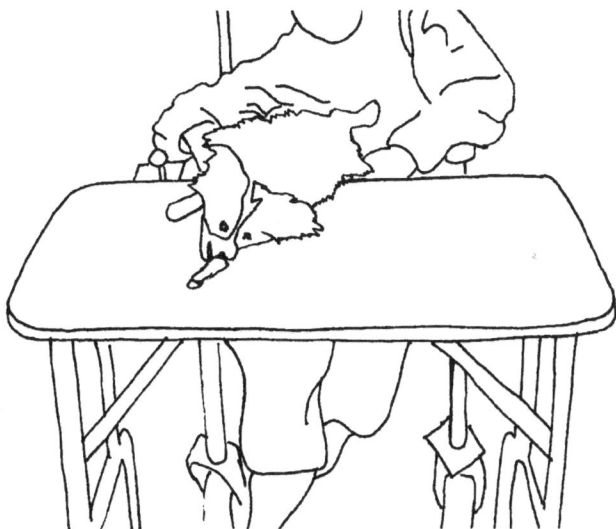

Your helper is only there to provide physical assistance. After the session your helper can play with the dog.

The dog must always be controlled on lead on the table. It is helpful if the table is placed in a corner so the dog can't fall off the left side or off the back. As she tries to get up to the food say, "up on the table" (dogs are capable of learning a short phrase).

When the dog can reach the food only by completely standing on the table, praise and give her a tiny piece of food in the standing position saying, "Stand, good, stand." Pet the dog while she is on the table before allowing her to get back into your lap. Repeat this pattern two or three times a day until the dog is really motivated to get up onto the table. Make the table a pleasant experience so that if you have to make future corrections on the table the dog won't associate these corrections with the table. While the dog is in your lap or on the table, stroke her in the manner previously described at least twice a day for 10-20 minutes. Spending time holding, stroking and giving special hot dog treats will create a bond that will continue to grow stronger as the training advances. When the dog is comfortable with being with you, and she begins to initiate this time spent together by following you around and seeking you out for attention, you can begin to teach her to come when called.

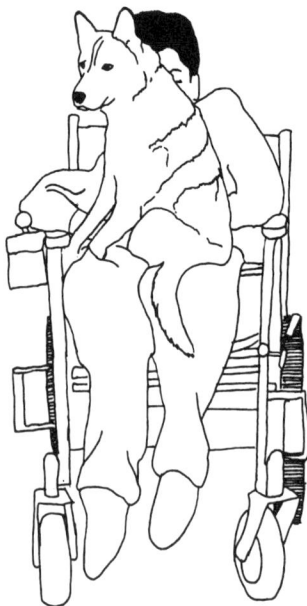

Comfort is a point of view!

Chapter Four

INFORMAL RECALL

One of my pet peeves is a dog with advanced training that cannot be trusted off lead. Before a dog is ready to compete in an AKC trial at the Novice level, she should be trained to the degree that she can exercise off lead in a field away from traffic, to run off a little anxiety from a training session or to just have a little doggy fun. That is not to say that I advocate letting a dog off lead near a busy street or in a potentially hazardous situation, or releasing an unreliably trained dog. You must use a little common sense.

Begin the informal recall in a quiet room of the house. I put a few hot dogs in my pouch. I use any type of collar on the dog with a 16' fully extended flexi-lead attached. I run my seat belt through the handle of the flexi so it is always accessible, leaving my hands free. The added advantage is that for formal recalls later on, the flexi will bring the dog into a straight front if looped on the center of my belt regardless of where my arms hang. When the dog wanders away, I call her by name. If she comes, I reward her with a tiny fragment of hot dog. If she does not respond immediately, I give her a jerk on the lead and reel her in. Then I treat and praise the dog. If you cannot physically give the jerk and you have a power wheelchair, let the chair give the jerk by rapidly moving in the opposite direction of the dog as you call. If this is not feasible, have your helper surreptitiously give the physical correction while you give exuberant praise to distract the dog from the helper. Remember, it is important that *the helper always remain silent* while you give all the commands and rewards. When the dog responds reliably to the first command, for two or three days, I introduce distractions. You can use another pet, another person petting the dog, or a roast beef on the coffee table! When the dog is otherwise engaged, call her to you, snap the lead and give her lots of exuberant praise and a treat when she comes. Coming always means coming close enough to touch, and the response should be immediate. Always make sure the dog is hungry before training. Never train her after a meal.

For the next level of training "the come" attach a 15' line to the dog's prong collar. This is called a longe line. If the dog is extremely neck sensitive to collar corrections use a choke collar. If you are in a wheelchair affix the end of the lead to the left armrest on the chair. I always manage to tangle myself in the line so I have a helper nearby. A double sided bolt snap hooked to

the handle of the line and around the armrest can facilitate easy removal of the line. If you are able to walk hold the handle of the line in both hands close to your body. You may also loop the lead around your waist if you have a small dog. The dog is now on a 15 foot slack line. Without giving commands or signals to

the dog, purposely head across the yard. Do not worry if the dog's feet get tangled. If you keep moving the dog will learn to untangle her feet all by herself. When the dog catches up to you, reward with a word of praise. I give the dog a moment to recover when I have reached my destination. I then head off in the opposite direction without speaking to the dog. Whenever the dog comes close enough for me to touch I give the "come" command rewarding with a small piece of food and a word of praise. As the dog begins to pay attention to where I am I begin making about turns and angled turns. I work around distractions and make swift about turns when the dog gets interested in something else. I continue to work around distractions rewarding with bits of food and praise when her attention is on me and she is close enough for me to touch. A small dog is encouraged to jump up on my knee to receive the food reward. When the dog is following me around the yard on the line I call the dog while backing up rewarding with food when she comes to me. You must condition the dog that coming to you will always be rewarded with food and praise. Try to catch the dog in every conceivable distraction so you can call the dog to you while you are still working her on the line. Only when you are convinced that the dog is totally reliable on the line you may begin working off the line. Call the dog to you when she is about ten feet away. Gradually increase the distance to where the dog will respond to you anywhere in the yard and under all circumstances. If you think your dog has the potential to work off lead in strange surroundings you may begin to try new places. Work only on lead using food and praise until you are absolutely convinced the dog will come to you before you go off the line. Work in safe, fenced areas until you have exhausted every possible distraction.

A dog that possesses an intense flight drive, which is a desire to run away, may need a shock collar. Some Northern, herding or sporting breeds are bred to run. You are fighting basic hereditary traits in dealing with sled dogs, live stock workers or hunting dogs. Mere food or a jerk on a collar cannot always override the urge of a strongly-bred instinct. I believe that a mild shock is a small price to pay for the future promise of freedom without getting hit by a car or being shot by a farmer protecting his livestock. Keep in mind that if you find it necessary to use a shock collar, have the dog wear it for several weeks before actually using it. Then she won't associate the correction with the collar, but rather with the act of running away. Be sure to study the available collars on the market and choose one that is lightweight, reliable and meets your distance requirements. This collar should never be used as a shortcut for good, sound obedience training and the correction should always be followed by overwhelming praise. I strongly advise working with a professional trainer knowledgeable in using shock collars. *Timing the shock is critical. Too many harsh corrections can ruin a dog forever.*

In a relatively short time you should have a reliable dog that will happily come to you off lead. You and your companion will enjoy many years of fun together.

I used to track with an obedience/tracking judge. We each had a Golden Retriever with obedience titles. After tracking her Golden, the judge had to leash her dog. She was afraid her dog would run off. Consequently her dog's reward for working a track was to be immediately put on lead.

After tracking my Golden, Chico, I was able to reward him by letting him off lead in the field to chase a ball or to play with the glove.

Chapter Five

TABLE TRAINING

While perfecting the informal recalls, you can spend a few minutes each day training on the table for small to medium dogs or on the bed for the larger breeds. If you wish to get one of the larger breeds of dogs, and you have limited arm or hand strength, I suggest starting with a 6-7 week old puppy that you can manage or an older dog already trained not to pull on the leash.

I use a small prong collar on all of my dogs because I have very limited muscular strength. I would use it, regardless of my ability, because somewhere down the line you may need it and the dog is already accustomed to wearing it. I never use it snugly as do most trainers. Instead, I keep it as loosely fitting as a buckle collar, with about an inch of slack. If I'm working a large, dog-aggressive dog, I double collar the dog. I attach the lead to the prong collar as well as to the choke collar, in case the links open on the prong collar.

When the dog is comfortable on the table, I hold a treat in front of her nose so she must stand to reach it. When the dog stands, I give her the treat. When the dog automatically stands when I position the treat I give the command, "stand." There is no point in giving the command until the dog is conditioned to standing when the hand holding the treat comes up to her nose. At this point, pull the treat forward so the dog must stand squarely to receive it. Repeat the command, rewarding with food and praise, when the dog is in the desired position. Any effort on the dog's part to lunge for the treat or to leap off the table is discouraged by a firm "No," a tug on the lead or, if necessary, a slap on the nose. *Having the dog fall off the table and breaking a leg does put a damper on the training session!*

I never have the dog examined during the stand at this stage. I prefer to begin stays and examinations in the sit position because it is easier to enforce.

I begin teaching the sit on my lap or on the table. This is so I can easily reach the dog and mold her into a correct, square sit. I can pet the dog and I can easily inspire eye contact at this level. Some dogs naturally watch your face, but others must be taught. I place an inch of hot dog between my lips and let the dog nibble on it. Teach the dog to be gentle so you don't lose a lip. *Use a brand of hot dog you enjoy for this exercise!*

If the dog is in my lap, my left hand grasps the dog's left leg at the hock. I gently but firmly push the leg forward under the dog, while my right hand holds the collar, thus preventing her from moving forward. I do not allow the dog to struggle while I hold her leg. Instead I hold the leg firmly, tell her "No" when she struggles and immediately praise her when she submits. This positions the dog into a quick tight sit.

As the dog sits, give the command, "Sit." Soon the dog will sit with just a light touch on the hock, and she will then progress to sitting on command. I use verbal and physical praise. No food reward is used for the sit as it is confusing with the stand, especially for conformation training.

The down is taught on the table by placing the hand, palm down, in the chain part of the prong collar positioned under the dog's chin. I slowly but firmly pull straight down immediately easing up on the collar once the dog is down. I scratch her chest and neck with my hand still in the collar while the dog is down.

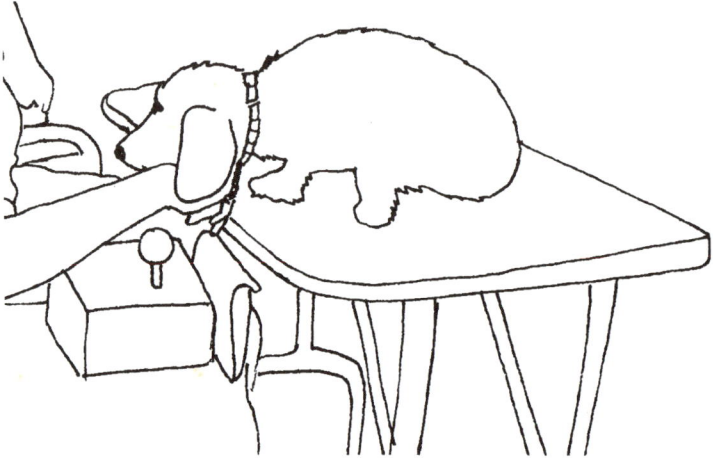

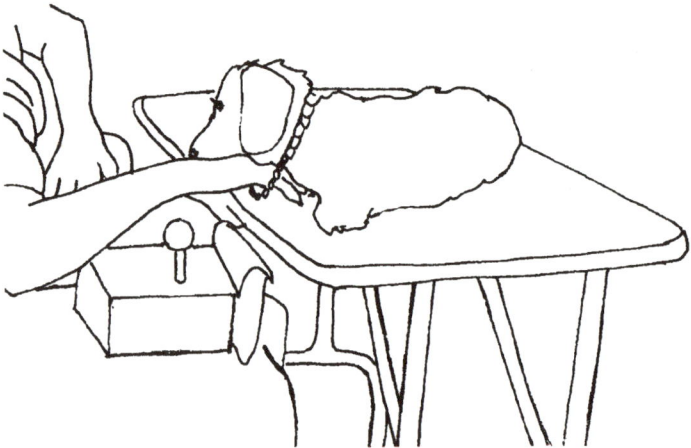

If you are unable to physically pull the dog down, you may use food. Hold the food in the same hand as the collar, enticing the dog down and feeding her while she is in the down position. Eventually try to eliminate the food. Get the dog accustomed to the collar correction. When the dog ceases to resist the pressure on the collar and will easily go down, I introduce the command "Down" as the dog *begins* to go down. Make sure you give plenty of verbal and physical praise when she goes down. Keep the dog down for several minutes while gently stroking her, slowly working up to keeping her in the down position for up to 10 minutes at a time. By having the dog next to you and close to the edge of the table, you can teach the dog to go down in a straight line without creeping. You should be able to train a quick response at this level because the dog is able to receive immediate physical rewards. Decreasing the distance between dog and trainer in any exercise enhances the timing of the correction and the reward.

At this point, you can begin teaching the sit and down stays. Do not allow the dog to get up or to move her feet. Gradually release the collar but keep your hand close to dissuade any attempt to move. Introduce distractions such as other people in the room, a ringing door bell, or preparation of the dog's meal. The dog is not allowed to move at all once the stay command is issued. From now on, "Stay" means to stay in place. When you simply want the dog to remain in an approximate location or not to go through a door or gate, use another command. I consider it inconsistent training to correct a dog one time for moving a paw and to let it slide the next time. Try not to issue a command that you are unable to enforce. Don't leave the dog on a stay and turn your back, especially before the dog is reliable. A slight shift of the body in the beginning can gradually lead to a major movement out of position later on. The stays create a wonderful opportunity to gain control over your dog. Take the time to teach it correctly and thoroughly in the beginning, and you will have fewer problems in your advanced training.

Once the dog is under control on the table and has learned to stand, sit, down and stay, grooming should be easier to accomplish. If you are unable to stand to groom your dog, she can be taught to remain in position for grooming while you are sitting. By using a grooming arm and two grooming loops, one loop attached around her neck and one looped around her

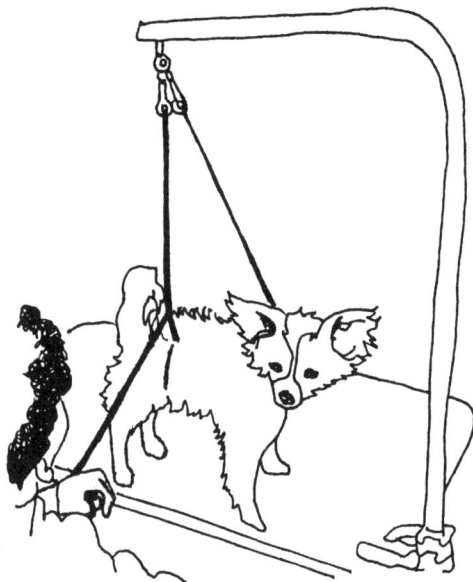

rump, you can keep the dog standing. If you need to turn the dog, connect a lead to the noose around the rump and you can propel the dog in any direction. Teach the dog "turn" so eventually you can eliminate the noose.

While the dog is in the correct position, reward her with gentle brushing and petting. Once the dog realizes that this is a pleasurable experience, she will gladly accommodate you. Off the noose you can get the dog to stand for grooming by gently pushing the brush with bristles or pins side up under the flank while saying "stand."

To trim the hair on the feet and the dog's nails, I begin with her right rear foot. I grasp the leg at the hock

and pull down with my left hand while my right hand is pulling down on the collar. This way the dog is lying down along the long side of the table. She is not allowed to move while you are grooming. Hold the foot firmly, correcting both verbally and physically if she moves. Do not attempt to groom until the dog accepts your physical manipulation of the foot. Once you trim the right rear foot, you can ease the left rear foot out from under the dog.

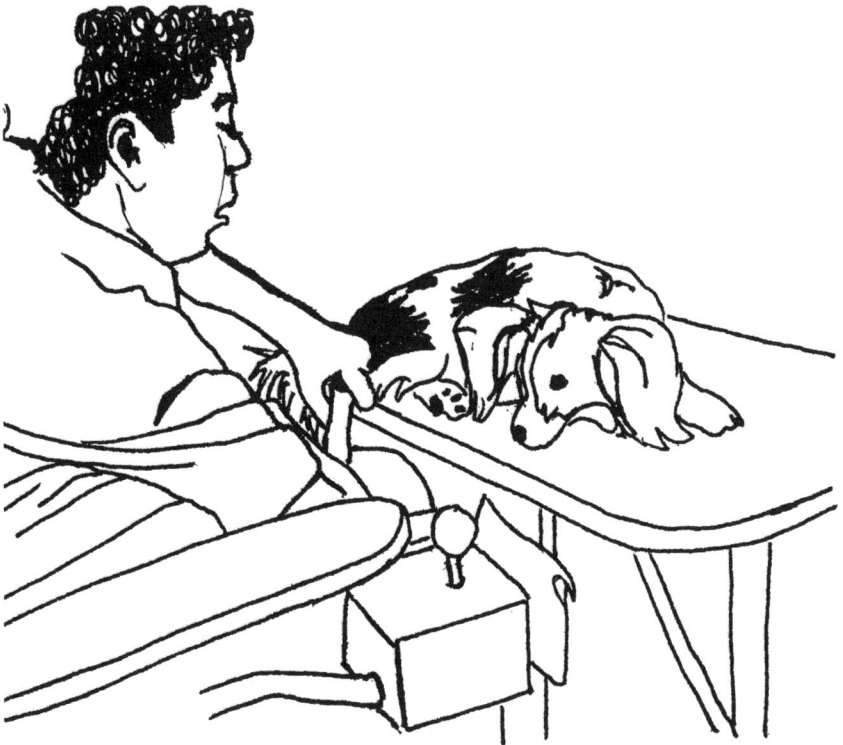

Hold the right rear leg in your left hand and with the same hand, and at the same time, ease the left rear leg toward you while pulling the dog's collar down with the right hand.

She will roll slightly over on her left side. After trimming this foot, you can teach the dog to roll over on her side before attempting to trim the front feet. This position is

one of submission for the dog. Many dogs are unwilling to lie on their side or back. You must begin training this as a young dog. Ask the breeder which puppies she can roll onto their back. A dominant dog does not easily submit to this position and is more difficult to train. I have had many dominant puppies that I could not turn over myself. I have helpers roll the dogs over for me and place them upside down in my lap while I calmly stroke the dogs' bellies. Fortunately, my large dogs have always enjoyed a tummy rub from my feet. They willingly flop over when I touch their flank with my foot when they are in the down position. Do not allow the dog to struggle or to get up on her own. Every time the dog wins the struggle, the next time you try will be even more difficult. If you or your helper do not know how to turn a dog over, ask your vet's technician to show you. When the dog is lying comfortably on her side, you can trim the front feet.

I trim whiskers for the show ring so I teach the dog to lie down facing me putting her head on my left wrist while I trim with my right hand. You can also use a small pillow or a rolled up towel for the dog to rest her

head upon. Other facial trimming or grooming can be done at this stage, except that I suggest you have someone else hold the dog's head while you clean ears. A sudden head flick, which can be purely an involuntary reflex, can cause serious ear injury.

Table training is the foundation for control and further advanced work. You should now be able to proceed to training on the ground level.

A make-over? Really, you'd think I was a Shar-Pei!

The first CH. UDT Papillon bitch was my beloved CH. Arbeitsheim's Choice Chablis UDT. "Chabby" was my devoted pet and companion as well as a wonderful obedience dog. She produced four litters and with each one she was a very loving and protective mother. After her final litter I bred another bitch called "Suki." Suki had four puppies that Chabby tried to claim as her own. I kept them apart but the inevitable day came when they met over the litter box. The result was that one of Suki's whiskers pierced Chabby's cornea during the ensuing fight.

The healing process took several weeks and countless painful treatments by the canine ophthalmologist. The vet would tell Chabby to "stand-stay" on the examination table and she would stoically accept her treatments without moving an inch. Chabby was a special dog but all of my dogs are welcomed patients by my vet because of their obedience trained stand-stays.

Chapter Six

LEAD BREAKING

Over the years my method of lead breaking young puppies has changed. In the old days I would put a collar and lead on a five to seven week old puppy and drag the puppy a few feet at a time until it would walk. I never considered that I was teaching my dogs to *crab* to my wheelchair. Crabbing is when the dog walks with the head toward you while the rear end swings out away from you. When I began to seriously exhibit in the breed and the obedience rings, I realized the importance of teaching the dog from the beginning to walk in a straight line.

I am unable to sit on the floor and play with my puppies, so at a very young age I put a lightweight breed lead on the puppy while I'm in bed watching TV. I pet and hold the puppy and when she begins to explore the bed, I restrain her with the lead. If she struggles against the lead, I pull her a few inches towards me and reward her with a bit of canned puppy food or hamburger. By the time she is five to six weeks I can get her to respond to the lead for the length of the bed. She is also being conditioned to come to me for food rewards. At seven weeks I can switch to very small amounts of hot dog. It only takes about an eighth of a hot dog per training session to condition a young puppy to food. When the puppy is no longer resisting the lead on the bed, I do the same lead training on the table.

At six weeks I have the puppy on the floor and I sit in my chair. When the puppy goes to the end of the lead, I pull her towards me and reward her with food. If the puppy is too short for me to reach, I drop the food at my feet. If the puppy is a large breed it is important to begin the training early. It is essential to me that I teach a larger breed puppy not to pull on the lead before she grows too big and too strong for me to handle.

I try walking the puppy alongside my chair on a straight sidewalk or curb. If the puppy has a tendency to walk in a straight line without getting under my wheels, I continue with short walks once or twice a day until she is satisfactorily lead broken. However, this is seldom the case.

I usually have to resort to a length of ½ inch PVC pipe either held in my left hand or clamped to the chair extended far enough away to keep the dog out from under the wheels. You can either run the lead through the pipe or drill a hole through the end of the pipe and attach the lead at the length needed to keep the puppy's head up and walking in a straight line. As the puppy grows, you will have to adjust the length of the lead.

If this method fails, I suggest having a helper lead break the dog. It is important that the helper walks in a straight line, keeping the head up, and being careful not to step on the puppy. The puppy will have ample time to learn how to avoid feet or wheels. Your job at this stage is to get the puppy confidently walking, head up, in a straight line by your left side. Take the puppy for short walks when the weather is not too hot or too cold, and always test concrete or asphalt to be sure it's not too hot for tender puppy feet. Avoid aggressive dogs or frightening situations for a puppy. Carry food to hand to strangers who stop to pet the puppy. I always ask willing strangers to feed my new dogs. If children stop to play with the puppy, instruct them to be gentle, and not to grab or rush at the puppy. Under no circumstances allow children or even most adults to pick up the puppy. A squirming puppy can easily fall from a person unaccustomed to holding a dog. I prefer to ask people to get down to the dog's level, which is far less threatening.

When the dog is confidently walking with the wheelchair and is no younger than twelve weeks old, I teach her to avoid the wheels. I do this on grass or carpet, making sure I can see the puppy at all times. I even use a mirror if necessary. I gently turn into the puppy, hitting her front feet only hard enough to teach her that not watching the wheels can be uncomfortable. I do this in a controlled situation where I am able to gauge the correction at the teachable moment.

My puppies quickly learn to avoid the wheels without injury. They get stepped on more often by my friends and helpers. Once this avoidance behavior is learned, you can use the longe line method as described in the informal recall chapter to teach the puppy to walk on a loose lead. This is vital for off lead heeling.

If my dogs are sleeping next to me they are signaled to get out of the way by the click of my wheelchair as it begins to move. Consequently I have a difficult time training my dogs to remain sitting in heel position when I leave them for recalls or the group stays. But on the positive side I never have to be aware of the location of my dogs because by being trained to avoid the wheels they are always aware of where I am. They have no fear of my chair and usually heel quite closely. I am forever being asked if I ever run over my dogs with the wheelchair. Depending on my mood at the time I often wickedly reply, "Only once."

Chapter Seven

THE SIT, DOWN, STAND AND STAY

Sit Stay

You have hopefully taught the dog to sit, down, stand and stay on the table or bed. If the dog is reliably responding to your commands with distractions present, the time has come to train on the floor. For all of this training I use the prong collar and a 6'x1/2" flat leather or cotton web lead. I use a heavy lead in all of my early training so that later on I can go to a very light-weight thin lead in preparation for off lead work.

The sit is taught separately from heeling. I teach the sit in front of me because I have more control. With the dog in front of me on the prong collar, I simply pull upwards until the dog sits. It may take a few patient moments, but I keep a taut lead until the dog sits. As the dog learns to sit from the pressure on the lead I give

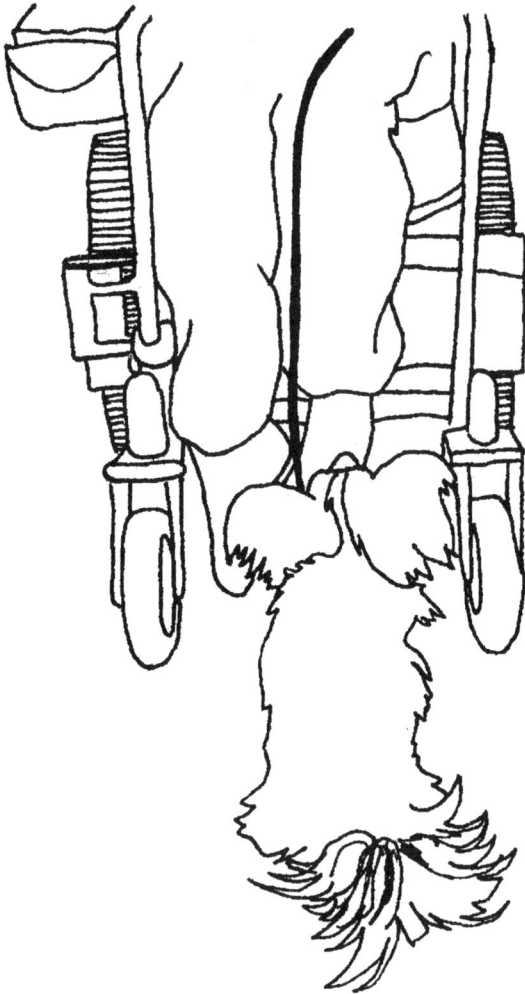

the command, "Sit" simultaneously with the lead correction.

Always remember to praise the dog when she responds correctly. Do five or six sits, two or three times a day until the dog is sitting instantly on the verbal command. To get an immediate response once you think the dog understands the command, a quick snap of the lead may be necessary. Release the pressure on the lead the instant the dog responds.

You may now teach the sit stay. This exercise may take a while to perfect because you will proceed slowly, building time and reliability in small increments. I sit the dog directly in front of me and say, "Stay." I carefully watch the dog for any shifting, which indicates she is preparing to get up. The moment she shifts or even *thinks* about shifting I give an emphatic "No," repeating "Stay." If the dog remains sitting I softly praise her. I build up the duration of the sit stay directly in front of me to 10 minutes over a period of several days. If the dog reliably sits for 30 seconds, I proceed to one minute. I then graduate to 2 minutes, then 3 minutes, then to 5, to 7, before working up to 10 minutes. I have people walking circles around the dog beginning 3 feet away and gradually moving in as close as possible without stepping on the dog. I have people touch the dog's head while she is on the sit stay, graduating to the point where they can examine her body without her moving a foot or tail. Only head movements are acceptable. I practice in shopping centers and around other dogs, cats, or even horses, and in front of automatic-opening grocery store doors. I think of as many safe distractions as I can at distances of several feet away, working them closer until the dog is confident and reliable. I never put the dog in a frightening or potentially dangerous situation. The dog must know that as long as she obeys you she can trust you to make sure that no harm will come her way.

I gradually move to a distance of 6 feet away from the dog at which time I pull gently on the lead. I move from side to side in preparation for the return to heel position. I begin to increase pressure on the lead while verbally and physically reinforcing the stay, to the

point where the dog is bracing her feet against the lead tension to maintain her stay position. I slowly return to the heel position a few inches at a time, praising constantly, until I can completely return. If the dog insists on getting up as I go behind her, I pass the lead to my helper who *silently* makes a collar correction by keeping the lead taut above the dog's head so she can't get up as I return. I work on this problem by having the dog sit stay while I am sitting directly behind her for a minute or two.

I gradually increase my distance from the dog on a flexi lead. Before I advance to out-of-sight sit stays, the dog must first be perfectly trained with me in sight. I begin out-of-sights by stationing a helper to look for any movement on the dog's part, and I briefly go in and out of the room before I leave for any length of time. In training I never ask a dog to stay when I'm not prepared to enforce the command. This rule of training significantly cuts down on the chances of the dog breaking a stay in a trial. Do not be afraid to praise your dog while she is maintaining the stay. You don't have to keep up a constant dialogue, but it is considerate to let her know that she is pleasing you.

When I show my toy breeds in trials, I always observe the dogs I know will be on either side of my dog on the group stays. If I think a dog is potentially dangerous to my dog I will tell the steward to inform the judge. I always have an able-bodied friend standing by the ring, especially on the out-of sight group stays. I instruct my friend to immediately step in and snatch up my dog at the first sign that my dog is in danger from another dog, either inside or outside of the ring. I always ask for additional space between my dog and those on either side in case one of these dogs shifts position or rolls over, so I have sufficient room to return to my dog. My dogs must not even move their tails so I can return safely. A wheelchair takes about two and a half feet of space from wheel to wheel. I also check for ants or bees in the grass before I place my dog on a long sit or down. If the temperature is exceedingly high, I wet the dog down so she is reasonably comfortable. Given all the precautions I take for the safety of the dog, I do not feel it unreasonable to ask her to maintain a 10 minute sit or down stay.

Down Stay

The down stays are trained and proofed exactly the same way as the sit stays. The trick is to get the dog to go down. When I teach a dog to go down, I have a picture in my mind of the way in which I want the dog to drop and the speed with which I want it executed. I do not settle for anything less, because later on, the drop on recall could be a problem in the advanced work. I want my dog to go down in a straight line without moving forward and as quickly as physically possible. A long-legged dog such as a Great Dane or Irish Wolfhound will probably not be able to drop as quickly as a Dachshund or a Sheltie. However, you can observe how the leggy dogs lie down naturally. Accept nothing less in training.

The dog has already had previous "down" training on the bed or table so it is reasonably familiar with the command and the collar pressure. Depending on the disability of the trainer and the size and strength of the dog, I have a few options for teaching the down.

My first choice is to have the dog in front of you. The dog is wearing a prong collar for all of these methods. Pass the lead under the instep of your foot pressing down while you are pulling up with the lead. If you need some extra leverage you can have the dog up on a curb or on a wide, high step. As before, you never issue the command until the dog understands the reason for the lead pressure.

My second choice is the use of a solid lead. You can either use a 1 inch PVC pipe or a wooden dowel with a bolt snap attached to one end. The bolt snap is attached to the prong collar and the stick should be of sufficient length to reach from your hand to the floor. You can push down on the stick to get the dog to go down.

My third choice is to drive a stake with a loop on top in the ground and run the lead through it. Back up pulling the dog down to the stake. You must have the dog directly over the stake to avoid teaching her to creep forward.

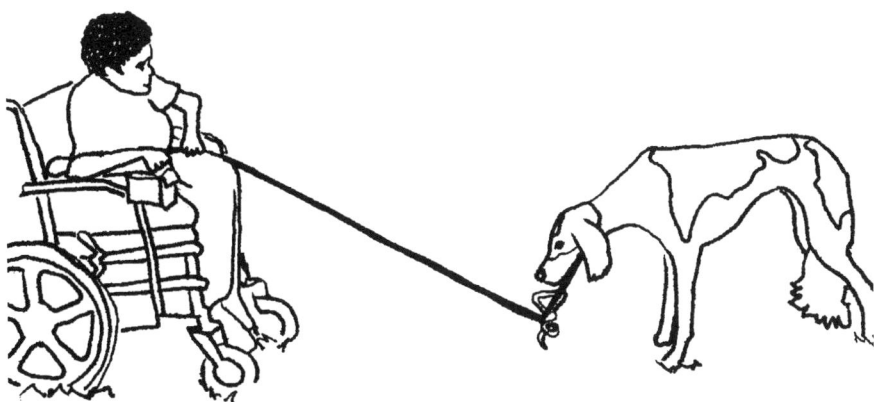

My fourth choice is to have a helper pull down on the collar while you drop a piece of food on the floor directly under the dog's nose.

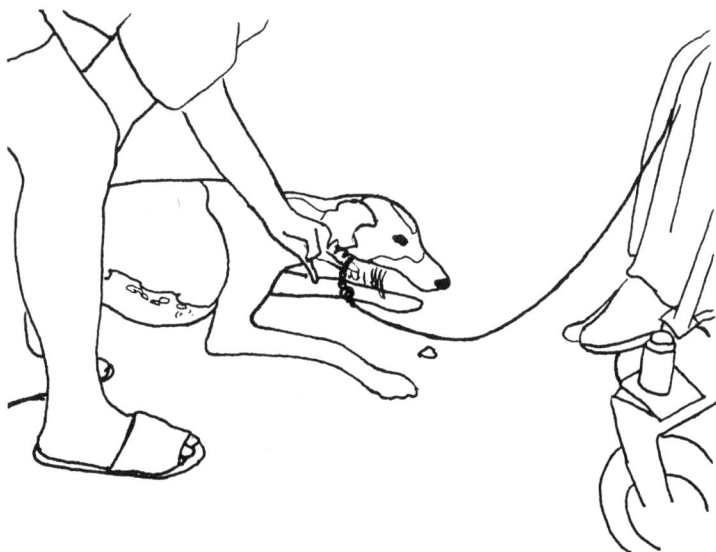

Hopefully, you'll find that one of these methods will work for you. But I would suggest introducing the down while the dog is young and not fully physically developed.

The Stand

The dog should be accustomed at this point to being examined on the sit and down by strangers. She should also tolerate your examination with either your hands or feet. You may also run a dowel against her body. Correcting a dog for moving during an examination is much easier on a sit or down, so she must be steady on these exercises before you attempt the stand for exam.

The dog has been taught to stand for food on the table and she should be familiar with "Stay" so the transition to the floor should not be too difficult. Holding a piece of food you can say "Stand" and gently walk or roll toward the dog until she stands. Another method is to run a lead under the dog's flank and pull up as you say, "Stand". Food is a useful tool to bait the dog into a comfortable, square stand. Do not give the stay command until the dog is standing squarely, to avoid the shifting of feet after you leave. The "Stand" command should sound distinctly different from the "Stay" command. The dog will learn to stand comfortably by herself when given the "Stand" command. During the length of time it takes for you to leave her, have her examined and return, she will become increasingly uncomfortable if she has not positioned herself correctly. If the dog moves or shifts a foot say, "No" and replace the foot to its original position. As a stranger approaches, remind the dog to stay. As you return to the dog remind her to stay again, until you feel that you can eliminate the extra stay commands. Teach the dog to resist a slight pull on the lead, which will teach her to plant her feet firmly. This will strengthen her reliability on the exercise.

When I began exhibiting in obedience, I did not realize I could ask for additional space on either side of my dog for the group stays. The judges, having never experienced a handler in a wheelchair, lined up all dogs and handlers quite closely. As a result, I inadvertently ran over my Chesapeake Bay Retriever's tail on the long sit. This caused a disqualifying score as well as a great deal of discomfort to the dog. Fortunately my next judge realized the problem. He suggested that before beginning the stays I ask the judge for sufficient room to return to my dog. The judges were always grateful for the suggestion.

When leaving your dog, even in practice make sure you have enough clearance to return. It is vital to teach the dog not to even move her tail, thereby taking up valuable space. But you must allow room for the dog next to you should its training not be as diligent as yours.

Chapter Eight

HEELING

Once the dog can walk on a loose lead, proper heel position can be taught. I use a 3 foot leather or flat cotton web lead. It is important to teach the dog to heel in a straight line before you incorporate turns or sits in heel position. I keep my lead taught so the dog is unable to move out of heel position while being careful not to force the dog's head into me, which creates crabbing. I hold a hot dog in my left hand with the lead and give the dog a treat every couple of steps. In the beginning I only have the dog walk a few steps

before I break the exercise, because at this point I am striving for accuracy and attitude. I only increase the number of steps when I think the dog is ready to progress. I keep just enough tension on the lead to keep the dog in correct heel position. When the dog is maintaining proper position, the lead tension is relaxed as the dog achieves the correct position. When she veers out of position, the lead self-corrects.

You need plenty of praise and intermittent food rewards to motivate the dog. You must maintain a straight line so the dog is confident that you won't bump into her, and you should proceed at a slow pace. The dog needs to learn to put one foot directly in front of the other while paying attention to where her body is in relation to you or your wheelchair. That concept involves a lot of concentration on the dog's part, and success is best achieved at a slow pace. Once the dog has mastered a few steps you may lengthen the distance to include a few more steps, until the two of you can heel successfully for about 50 feet. Remember to motive the dog by giving her enthusiastic praise and a treat every few feet. You may test the dog's accuracy by releasing the tension on the lead every once in a while to see if she maintains the position by herself.

When you can successfully heel for 50 feet in a straight line, you may introduce the sit in heel position. Try heeling along a wall or fence. Take a step or two, halt and say "Sit" while pulling up on the lead. If the dog was in proper heel position when you stopped, chances are that you will get a decent sit. Don't worry about perfection at this point. You simply want the dog to sit when you stop. When the dog sits, give her praise and a treat. Work on the sit every few steps, being careful not to make the exercise monotonous for the dog. Vary the number of steps that you take between sits, and break the exercise with lots of exuberant praise. Practice this for only a couple of minutes each time, and only when the dog is fresh. It's a good idea to keep the dog crated away from you for at least 30-60 minutes before practicing this exercise. When the dog grasps the concept of the sit at heel, you can proceed to shape the sit for a faster and more accurate response.

A quick jerk release on the prong collar will elicit a faster sit. An accurate response can be achieved by giving food only when the dog sits straight.

Another way to help the dog understand the concept of sitting straight at heel is the left quarter turn pivot. To teach left quarter turn pivots, I back my chair to the left. The lead is kept short and tight. I say "Back" and back up to the left at a 45 degree angle. If the left front wheel is not straight when I complete the pivot, I move slightly forward to straighten the wheel. If I were walking, it would be a neat military left turn with an immediate halt after the completion of the turn.

When teaching the right turn, I keep the lead tight, encouraging the dog to keep up by using food and verbal encouragement. Avoid letting the dog charge into the turn, resulting in a forged position. Execute all turns slowly in the beginning so as not to confuse the dog. Achieving a straight sit after a right turn is more difficult than on a left turn but it can be accomplished with a bit of patience and practice. You can help the dog sit straight on a right turn by practicing alongside a wall or fence.

I practice heeling and sits with a mirror. Eventually the dog learns to sit accurately when she sees herself in front of the mirror so I ask friends to observe my dog's accuracy while heeling and quietly say "Yes" or "No" depending on the quality of the sit.

If the dog is sitting with his rear out or crabbing while heeling, I use a 3' x 3/8" dowel to tap in her rear end. You must acquaint the dog with the dowel first by slowly rubbing it along her body. Don't let her avoid the stick or pull away. Make it a pleasurable experience and never hit her with it.

Acquainting the dog with the dowel

About turns are extended right turns. A wheelchair is much wider than a person's feet, so pay attention to the way in which you execute your turns so you don't leave your dog trailing behind you. Concentrate on being consistent on your turns so that the dog knows what to expect.

Changes of pace should have a smooth transition. If you use a wheelchair, remember that your chair handles differently on grass than on slippery indoor matting. Practice without the dog on both surfaces. Sometimes the chair gathers up the mats on a turn or on a change of pace, and the dog ends up sitting or heeling on a wrinkle. Your chair will respond differently on halts depending on the surface. You can warm up on grass before entering the ring at outdoor trials, but you are not afforded the luxury of a matted ring on which to practice at indoor trials. Therefore, you must take advantage of the few feet you travel from the ring entrance to the place where the judge begins the heeling pattern. Heel your dog to that spot, and when you halt you can determine how your chair reacts to the surface. This is your only chance to remind the dog to sit. Make use of the opportunity.

When performing the figure 8, if you elect to go to the left first, position your chair slightly to the right of the center of the posts to give your dog room to properly negotiate the turn. You can't require the posts to be any wider apart than a normal figure 8. You may ask the judge to reposition the posts to give sufficient clearance from jumps or ring gates.

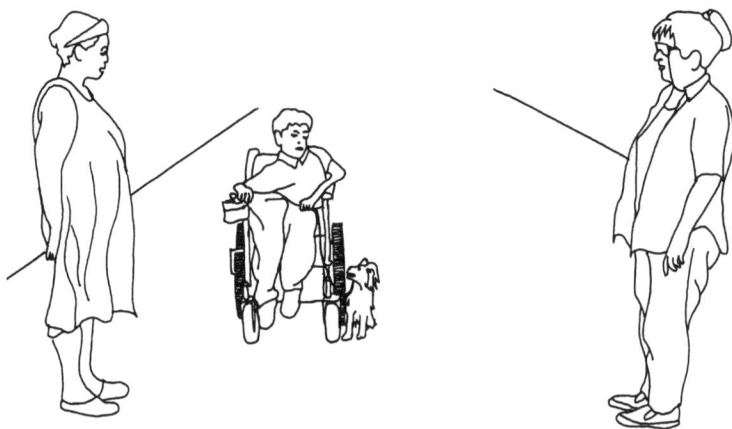

You are ready for off lead heeling *only* when your dog is consistently performing on a loose lead without the aid of the prong collar and is maintaining heel position in all types of distracting situations.

To facilitate the transition to off lead heeling I use a light line. If I'm working a toy dog, I use fishing line. A medium dog can wear a thin nylon cord, and a large breed can do with a slightly heavier nylon cord. Use the lightest possible clip or simply tie a slip knot onto the choke collar. I tie the cord to the left arm of my chair leaving about 12 inches of slack measured to heel position, or you may tie it around your waist if you are walking. If the dog is short, tie the line lower on the frame of the chair or lower on your leg using 6 inches of slack. Do all of this before you slip the choke collar on the dog so you don't alert her to the idea that she is attached to the line. Snap her regular lead to the collar and do a minute of warm-up heeling. Either you or a helper will then remove the regular lead in such an obvious manner to the dog that she thinks she is off lead. If your helper removes the lead, have her pet the dog so she is distracting the dog away from you. If you remove the lead, give the dog a release command. Before the dog can take up the slack in the light line, give an authoritative heel command and swiftly head off in the opposite direction. The dog will be quite surprised at the correction. Do about a 30 second heeling pattern while enthusiastically praising the dog, and then snap on her regular lead. Continue this training pattern for several days slowly increasing the amount of time spent heeling on the light line until you are able to complete about 5 minutes of satisfactory heeling. You will find that the dog's attention will become riveted to you when her regular lead is removed. When you are finished training, remove the collar. Don't fumble around trying to remove the line from the collar. Simply remove the collar with the line attached. The dog will learn to associate the collar with her obedience work, especially heeling.

The transition to off lead heeling is accomplished in the same manner as used with the light line. Remove the light line before you put the collar on the dog and attach her regular lead to the collar. Practice a 30 second warmup heeling pattern on lead. Remove the lead, give the heel command and take off in the opposite direction. If the dog is heeling satisfactorily, continue off lead for about a minute. If the dog is making mistakes, she goes back on lead for several sessions. Always end your off lead work with a few minutes of on lead reinforcement. If the dog is bolting while off lead or is not heeling with you, chances are that you went off lead before she was ready. Teaching a dog to heel properly on lead takes many months of dedicated training. It is, however, worth the time and effort because if the dog ever understands how little control you have off lead, your teamwork is doomed. Some dogs are unsure of themselves off lead and will gain confidence by using very short training sessions and an abundance of praise and food rewards. You will need to alternate between lead, light line and off lead work for quite some time. The art of training is being able to read your dog. You need to evaluate her understanding of each exercise and decide whether she is ready to advance to the next level of training. You must be able to determine whether the dog is confused or is just being obstinate. If you advance your training prematurely or stay at one level too long, the results can be quite detrimental. Hopefully you and your dog are developing a good working relationship at this stage of your training.

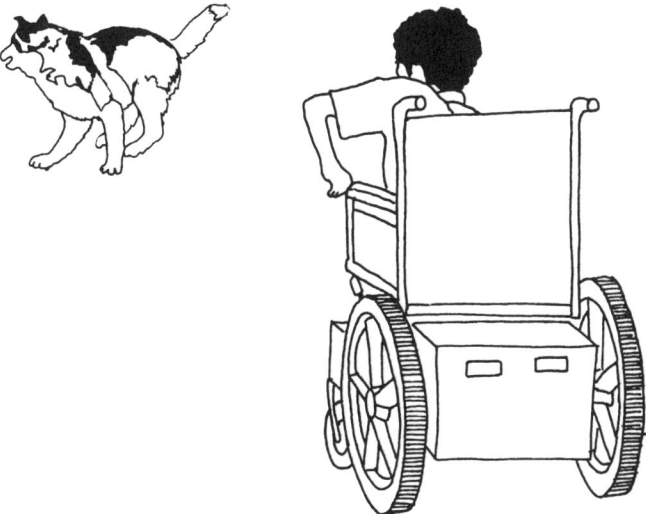

Losing control.............

Because of my training methods for off lead heeling I can, for the most part, depend on my dog to respond well in the obedience ring. The dogs are used to having their leads removed by my helpers while I am controlling them with a light line. I have further insured my reliability on off lead ring work by having my helpers act like ring stewards. They remove the lead while petting and speaking sweetly to my dogs. Real stewards don't understand how distracting this can be for diverting attention away from the handler. I use this to my advantage because as soon as my helper unsnaps my lead I say "heel" and give a firm snap on my light line heeling away from the helper who may still be touching or speaking to the dog. By the time my dog is ready for Novice competition she is trained to think that the stewards removal of the lead is a set up for an off lead correction. As soon as the lead is removed I command, "Heel" and wheel off to the spot for the stand for exam. This cue of the presence of the judge and steward serves to really focus my dog on her off lead work. So a word of thanks to all of these wordy, hands on touching stewards out there who have helped me earn those placements. Remember - NO TRAINING IN THE RING!

Chapter Nine

THE RECALL

I use the word "Front" when I want the dog to sit straight in front of me. The command, "come" means to come in the general vicinity of my body. "Front", means a straight position between the front wheels of my chair, close enough to look up into my face and to deliver the dumbbell without having to step forward.

To teach the front exercise, the collar is placed under the chin with a 3 foot lead attached. You can use either a prong collar with the chain under the chin or a choke collar on the dead ring. The dog should be accustomed to being fed and petted near your feet. Remember that you are sitting in a wheelchair, so the perspective from the dog's point of view is entirely different than if you were standing. If you are training a dog for a person in a wheelchair, you should sit in their chair to teach accurate fronts. The front wheels should always be straight and parallel to each other. I use food and only give it to the dog when she is in the desired front position. I use the collar and lead to motivate the dog towards me, and I use my feet to guide the dog into the straight front. I do not use the foot rests on my chair, but if you are unable to use your feet the use of the footrests might be a handy guide.

With the dog sitting or standing in front of me, I put a piece of food between my knees and I position my feet on either side of the dog like a chute. If the dog is a large breed, you don't have to use your feet. I back up while guiding the dog into a straight sit, using the command "Front". I only back up sufficiently to get the dog to come in straight. This is not a recall but is merely a "Front" exercise. When the dog is straight and close, I pull up on the lead and say "Sit". If you get a quick sit the dog should be sitting straight. If the dog twists her body off to one side at the last moment, back up and pull straight up on the lead until she sits straight. You reward the dog only when she is in the proper position and give her food from between your knees. If the dog is taller than your knees, put the food in your mouth. I suggest using a brand of hot dog that you enjoy, as this concept takes a bit of time and training for the dog. As the dog's accuracy improves, you can back up slowly for longer distances of up to 30 feet which is the distance of a formal recall. This teaches the dog to put one foot directly in front of the other teaching her to walk in a straight line toward you. Don't work on the speed of the recall now, just the accuracy. The speed will come later. Since the dog will also have to learn to come to the front position from an angle, you will have to teach this concept. With the dog sitting in front of you, give the "Stay" command and go offside to the right a few feet. Command "Front" and move back until the dog is straight. Practice this from both offside rights and offside lefts. Some dogs have a preference, so you must work harder to train the direction to which they have the most difficulty adjusting. Even when you think the dog understands "Front", it is an exercise you will constantly have to review.

When the dog understands the "Front" command when you are backing up, leave the dog on a sit stay about 6 feet away and call her to front while you remain stationary. Point to the front position between your knees and have a food reward ready. Reel the dog in with your lead to get a straight sit.

The next step is to use the longest flexi-lead you can manage. I run my belt through the handle of the flexi thus leaving my hands free. I have already taught the dog to resist the drag on the flexi as I leave her on a sit stay. Even a toy dog can sit stay while you leave and let the line pull out. I find it easier and faster than pulling out the slack as I leave the dog with the added advantage of reinforcing the stay. Before you call the dog front give her a foot of slack, so when you release the flexi she gets a snappy correction which will bring her in at a faster pace. If the flexi is looped through your belt, you should get a pretty decent front. If it is not straight, back up just enough to straighten up the dog *before* she sits. When the dog is coming towards you say "Sit" about two feet before she arrives, which will remind her to sit in front. If the flexi is bringing her in fast and straight, a quick reminder to sit just before she reaches you will help insure a straight sit. Reward with a food treat. When the dog is executing an accurate fast recall on a long flexi, you may introduce distractions. Have a helper pat the dog on the head as you call her, or have a helper attempt to distract her with food. You may have a helper walk by with another animal. You can also practice in a busy shopping center. The dog will soon realize you are going to correct her to you when she pays attention to the distractions, and she will begin to really focus on you. Do not allow her to look away from you when you are training which will hopefully prevent her attention from wandering at a trial.

When you are ready to go off lead, begin at distances of six to ten feet. Use intermittent food rewards for a straight front, and don't hesitate to solve any relapses by going back to your lead or to the flexi.

Chapter Ten

THE FINISH

The finish is always taught to the left of the wheelchair as you do not want a dog on lead crossing to the right and coming around the back of the chair. You must also teach the dog to go back far enough so that she will be parallel to the chair when she makes her turn.

I generally begin teaching this exercise two feet from a wall on my left. I hold the lead taut in my left hand with the dog

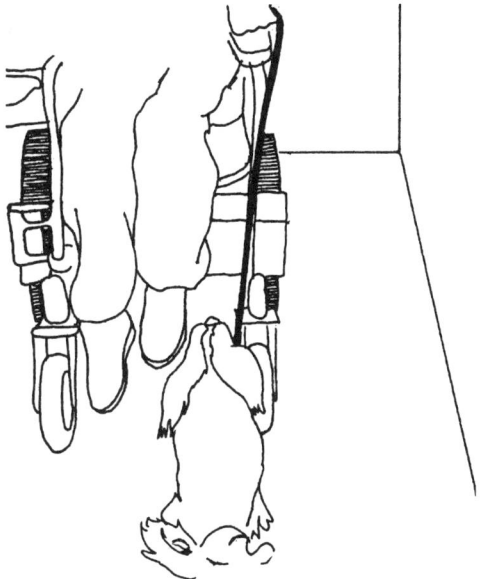

sitting slightly to the left of the front position. As I tell the dog to heel, I pivot back on my left wheel pulling the dog to the left between the wall and my chair. When the dog is back far enough to turn, I straighten up parallel to the wall while telling the dog to sit when she is in heel position. The wall guides the dog into a straight sit while at the same time teaching her to make a close, tight turn. At first the dog may shy away from working close to the wall, but you must be firm about this. Soon you will be able to move even closer to the wall depending on the size of your dog. If you find that further on in training the finish that your dog refuses to go to heel unless you move, you have three options.

The first choice is to hold the lead taut in your left hand off to the left side of the chair with the dog sitting directly in front of you. Tell the dog to "Heel", and move the chair rapidly forward. Hopefully the dog will move out of the way, as your lead gives her no alternative but to flip to heel position. You may sit the dog with

her back a foot away from a wall so she can't move
back as you move forward.

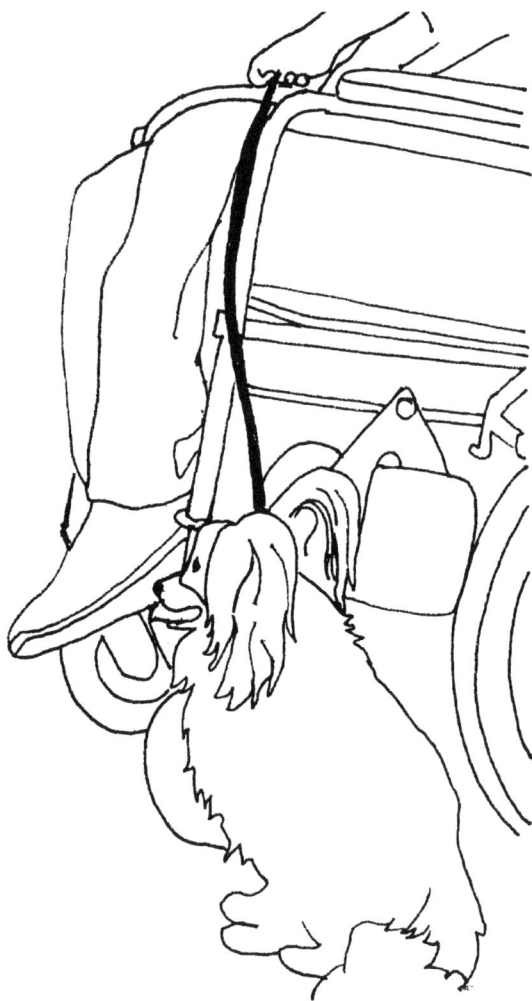

If the brain child hasn't gotten the concept after a realistic amount of time and you still feel like keeping her instead of giving her to your sister, you might try the second option.

Use a three foot dowel or PCV pipe with a bolt snap secured to the end and attached to the collar. This is referred to as a solid lead. Pulling this lead toward your left side while you remain in place may give you some leverage in getting the dog into heel position.

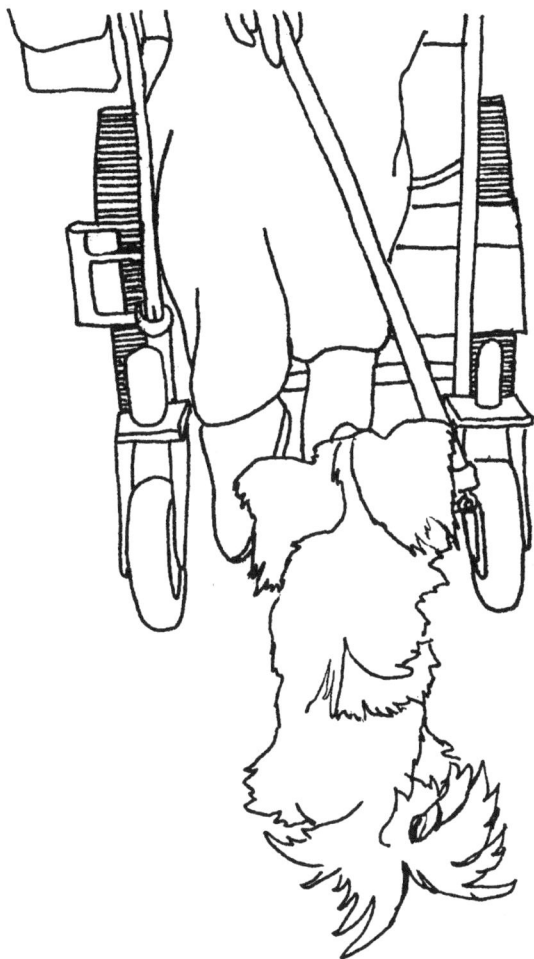

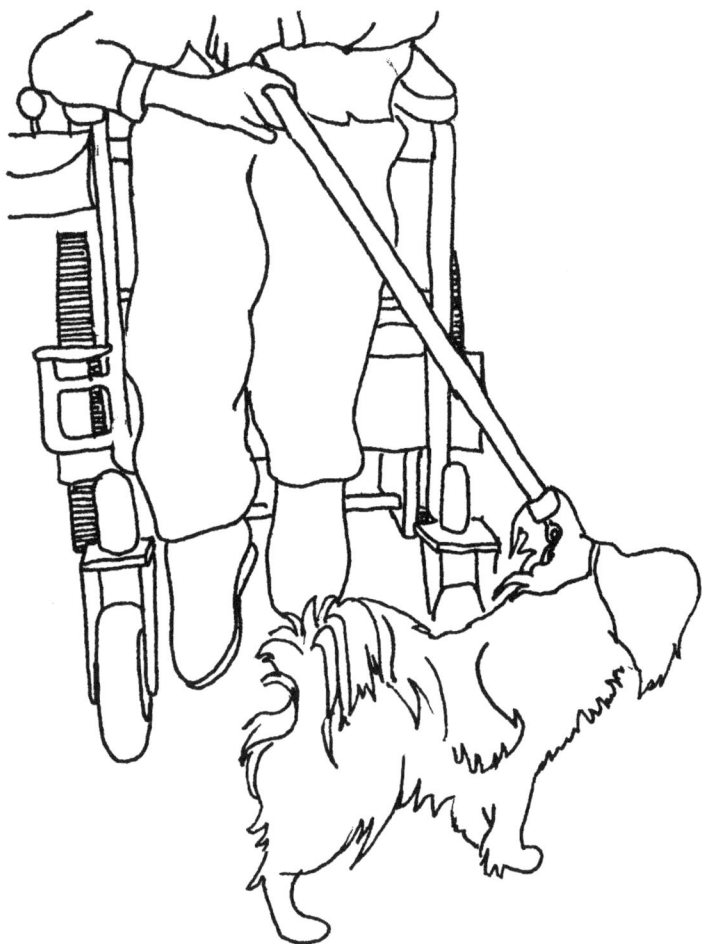

If you are unable to handle the solid lead, the third option is to enlist your helper. Hold your lead without slack off to the left side with the dog sitting in front. Attach a second lead to the dog of a sufficient length that will allow your helper to stand several feet behind you. The helper will use the second lead to pull the dog to your left on your command to heel. As soon

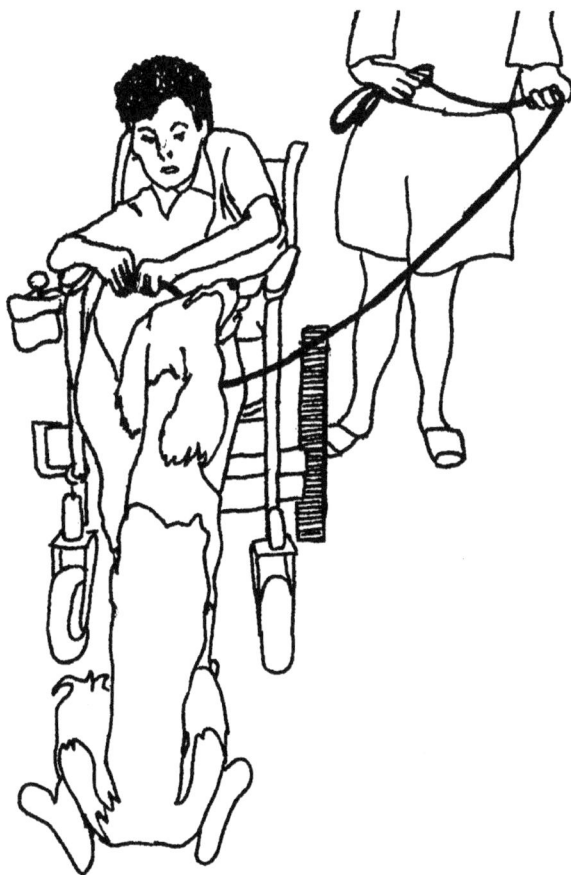

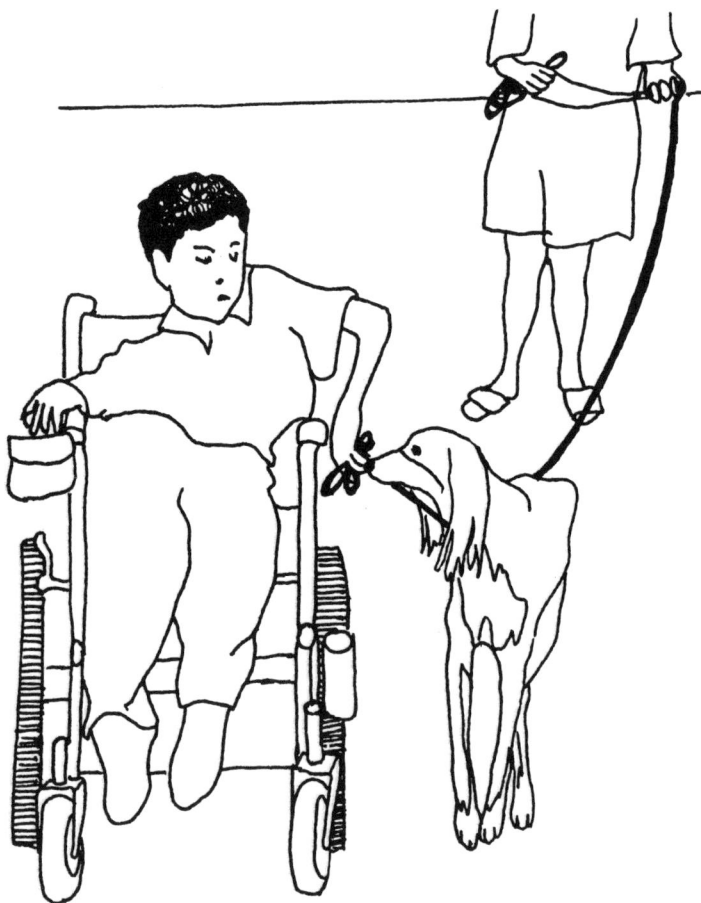

as the dog goes back far enough, use your lead to turn
her and bring her into heel position. Reward the dog
with food when she sits in proper heel position.

Because the dog may anticipate the finish if combined too soon with the recall, I would suggest keeping the exercises separate in the beginning of training. When the dog is executing a rapid recall and she knows front position you may begin to add an occasional finish. Alternate ending the exercise with the "Finish" and giving enthusiastic verbal praise and release on completion of the "Front". Even when you are practicing for competition I advise that you often end the exercise with the recall.

If the dog slows up on the recall, work on regaining the speed. Give the dog a sit stay, show her a piece of food and quickly move to the 30 foot required distance. Call the dog to you while rapidly backing up several feet. Reward the dog with food as soon as she approaches close enough to receive the food. Do not use the command "Front" because you are not requiring a sit front. When the dog builds up her speed you may then give her a sit stay, show her the food, call "front" and back up rewarding with food on completion of the sit in front.

If you are experiencing difficulities with the sit front position, return to your original teaching of the front exercise. Do short, motivational fronts using food, mild collar corrections and lots of verbal praise.

Incorporate finishes when the dog is proficient on the rest of the recall exercises but continue to alternate the way in which you end the exercise *before* the dog begins to slow down, loses front position or anticipates the finish.

By using food and praise to motivate the speed of the recall you may have to occasionally reinforce the sit stay. Leave the dog on a sit stay, go to the end of the recall, wait a brief moment and return to the dog. Reward the dog with verbal and physical praise for remaining on the stay. At all times you should work by breaking down the sequences of the recall and continueously work on speed and accuracy while preventing anticipation of the finish.

Chapter Eleven

THE RETRIEVE

Before you begin my method of teaching the retrieve I suggest that you read William Koehler's method of the force retrieve as outlined in his Open Book of Dog Training. Although our methods differ slightly, the concepts of using force, proceeding in small increments and training with distractions to insure a reliable retrieve, are exactly the same. I have adapted Mr. Koehler's techniques to accommodate my disability and you, in turn, can change my methods to suit your needs. But without Bill Koehler's original concept, I would not have been able to train six dogs to the Utility title. If you take the time to properly train a dog to retrieve an obedience dumbbell, why not make the extra effort to teach the dog to pick up useful items for you? My retrievers could pick up a dime off the floor and drop it in my lap, and my Papillons will pick up my mail and bring it to me. My trained dogs lie by my feet, anticipating the moment that I drop something so they can fetch it for me. The dogs are thrilled to perform this task for me and their help is very important to my independence.

The *delivery* of the retrieve object is a very difficult concept for the dog. My large breeds have to position the item on my lap so I can take it. I have a very limited reach. The dumbbell or any object must be presented at my level and at just the right angle and held there until I can grasp it with my right hand. My retrievers were already at the correct height for my reach while sitting in front but even if they came in straight, they had to stretch their heads forward and lay the dumbbell in my lap. My Papillon has an even more difficult task. In a trial she must pick up the dumbbell and return to a sit in front. Upon the command to release it, the dog must rise up to my lap with the dumbbell angled toward my right hand. Once I take the dumbbell, the dog must return immediately to a straight sit in front without an additional command. If I am asking the dog to retrieve other objects as well as a dumbbell, she must figure out how to present each object so I may easily reach it. A dog must be very reliable in the training of the hold to be able to do this, and a play retrieve doesn't always do the job. In the beginning of teaching a play or food-motivated retrieve you must be able to easily reach down and take the object from the dog's mouth before she drops it. My dogs must reach up and place the object close to my hand.

I am unable to throw the dumbbell a significant distance. The dog must wait until I go out, place the dumbbell and return. My dog must stay in place longer than my competitors and remember the place where I dropped the dumbbell until she is sent. When performing the high jump she must go over the jump instead of going around as I did when I placed the dumbbell. A toy dog's dumbbell is often difficult to see at a distance in the grass, so the dog must concentrate on going out in a straight line and not giving up until she finds it.

Now that we understand the difficulties that the dog will encounter, we need to learn how to reliably train the dog to willingly and confidently perform her job. Once a dog has learned to reliably retrieve for you, her devotion and trust will be unmistakable. It is a good idea to hold off showing in Novice until the dog has been taught to retrieve because of the ultimate bonding you will experience by using the forced retrieve. The dog will also be able to retrieve her lead and armband for you after the long down. All initial training of the retrieve is taught with a dumbbell, because the shape is easier for the dog to hold and for you to handle. Use a size that is comfortable for both of you. The dog can adapt far easier to what she is able to pick up than you can adapt to what you can easily hold and reach.

With large breeds I begin the training early for obvious reasons. If your dog is already older and too strong for you to manage, you will need help. Having someone else train the dog for you will not diminish her desire to work for you. The idea is to get the training over quickly and efficiently so that the dog has success at each step of the training process. Small dogs are started in my lap. With any size breed you are going to need help when you are ready to go down to the floor, so you may as well enlist your helper from the beginning.

The Hold

I begin the retrieve by teaching the dog to hold the dumbbell. Depending upon the nature of the dog, this can sometimes be the most difficult part of the exercise. I observed that my friend's American Staffordshire Terrier had no difficulty with the hold concept due to his jaw structure and his natural instinct to hold his prey, but he had to be taught not to "kill" or shake it. Some Papillons love to chase an object but disdain holding it in their mouth for any length of time. Each dog is different, and some will progress more rapidly than others during each step of the training process.

I open the dog's mouth by pressing her lips under the canine teeth. If she objects to this, I concentrate on just getting her to open her mouth. I do not allow her to struggle or to move out of my reach. I either have a short, thick lead on her or I hook my left hand under the buckle or chain of the prong collar. A choke collar has too much play in it so I do not use it at this stage of training. I continue working on getting the dog to accept my opening her mouth. When I am able to easily open the dog's mouth without any objection from her, I place the dumbbell behind the canine teeth and command "Hold".

The dog need not hold the dumbbell for more than five seconds, but during that time she must hold it securely without rolling, chewing, or attempting to spit it out. Your job is to prevent the dog from forming any of these bad habits at this stage. As soon as you place the dumbbell in the dog's mouth and command "Hold," you lightly wrap your hand around the muzzle so she cannot shift the dumbbell. While you are silently

counting to five, you should be praising softly. When you want the dog to release the dumbbell say, "Out," ease up on the pressure on the muzzle, and take the dumbbell by the bell from the dog's mouth. You may give a brief word of praise when the dog takes the dumbbell but she should be continuously praised while she is holding it. If the dog attempts to mouth or spit out the dumbbell, grasp the muzzle firmly and say "Hold it" in an authoritative tone of voice. When the dog is doing a proper hold, ease up on the muzzle and give praise in a soft, soothing tone. You should practice this step about ten times in a row three times a day. You are ready to increase the length of time the dog is required to hold the dumbbell when she is perfectly holding it without any resistance for five seconds. Increase the hold time until the dog is holding for one minute and you are able to fully remove your hand from the dog's muzzle. You may then use that hand to gently stroke her on her chest while praising softly. This induces the dog to relax while holding the dumbbell for longer periods of time. When the dog is steady on the hold, apply a little pressure on a bell of the dumbbell to remind her to continue her hold. Grasp one end of the dumbbell but do not allow the dog to give it up except on the "Out" command. Then progress to gently tugging on the end of the dumbbell with one hand while holding her mouth closed on it with the other hand, preventing the dog from releasing the dumbbell prematurely. The dog should be able to maintain a steady hold on the dumbbell while a fair amount of pressure is applied. Once you have mastered a one minute hold right next to you, put the dog on a chair if she is small, or on a sit stay on the ground, and reinforce the hold with distractions.

Use distractions as previously described in the sit and down stays. Travel to playgrounds or shopping centers where there is a lot of noise and activity.

You may then progress to the point where you can leave the dog on a sit stay and go around her to heel position, then return in front to take the dumbbell. When the dog is proficient at this stage, the next step is to teach her to walk while holding the dumbbell. *Just as with some people, it is difficult for some dogs to walk and chew gum at the same time!*

With the dog holding the dumbbell in front of you, slowly back up a few steps and call the dog to you. Position the collar and lead under the dog's chin so the lead can help keep the bottom jaw from opening, thus

preventing the dumbbell from dropping. Remind the dog to "Hold," and praise her while she is walking toward you.

Do not allow the dog to mouth or drop the dumbbell. When she has successfully walked a few steps toward you, give exuberant praise and take the dumbbell. If you are training a small dog you may place the dog on a card table, a long picnic table or bench. At this level you can easily reach the dog thus preventing mistakes. Gradually increase the distance a few feet at a time until the dog can cheerfully travel at least 30 feet on or off lead, without any thoughts of chewing, rolling or dropping the dumbbell.

At this point your dog should be reliably holding and carrying the dumbbell on or off lead while ignoring distractions. You have laid the foundation for the retrieve. You are now going to apply some kind of force to get the dog to open her mouth. The technique you use will depend on the dog's threshold of pain and your ability to effect a swift, forceful correction. I use either an ear pinch or a collar twist. To do the ear pinch, I hook my fingers in the collar except for my thumb which I use inside the ear to give the correction. The dumbbell is ½ inch from the dog's mouth at this stage of training. Upon the command to fetch, the thumbnail is quickly pressed inside the ear. As the dog opens her mouth, the dumbbell is inserted and the ear pressure is

immediately released. The dog is heartily praised after which you give the "Out" command and remove the dumbbell. The dog doesn't have to hold the dumbbell for more than a brief moment while she is learning to reach for it. The key to an effective ear pinch is that the force should be swiftly applied when you issue the command, and it should be stopped immediately when the dumbbell is in the dog's mouth.

When the dog is consistently opening her mouth on the fetch command, you hold the dumbbell one inch from the dog's mouth and do not release the ear pinch until the dog moves her head towards the dumbbell and grabs it on her own. You do not place the dumbbell in the dog's mouth, it is now up to the dog to reach for it herself. It is your responsibility to time your correction so the pressure is applied upon the "Fetch" command and released when the dumbbell is in the dog's mouth. Faulty timing or slow, drawn out pressure on the ear is unfair to the dog and is usually the reason for the failure of this method.

If you can effect a collar twist more efficiently that technique is also acceptable. You can even use a prong collar for this if your muscular ability is limited. The collar is placed high up under the dog's chin and the twist is applied high on the back of the neck between the dog's ears. The twist is given in a rapid motion and is immediately released when the dog opens her mouth and grabs the dumbbell. The progression used to get the dog to reach for the dumbbell is exactly the same using either the ear pinch or the

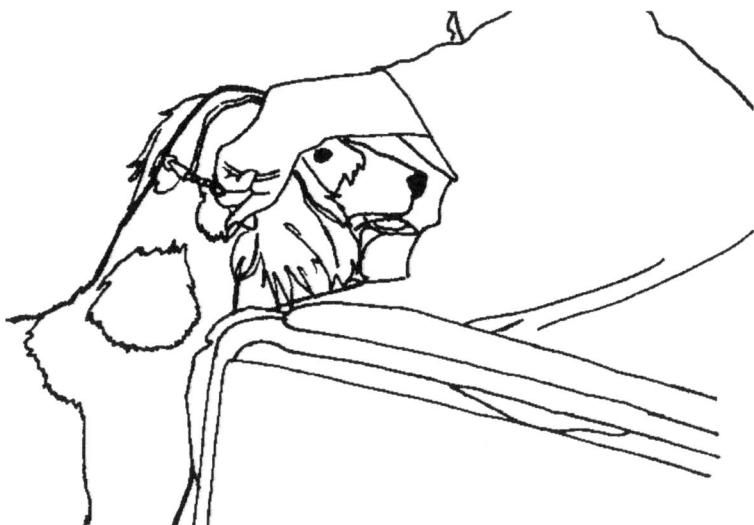

collar twist. Move the dumbbell a small distance from the dog's mouth only when she is successfully reaching from inches away and in distracting situations. Remember, it's very important to not move the dumbbell toward the dog, but to motivate the dog to reach for the dumbbell.

I can not stress enough the importance of effecting the correction as quickly as possible upon issuing the command and releasing the pressure just as quickly once the dog has the dumbbell in her mouth. If you use this method for short sessions of 10 retrieves three times a day, and only increase the distance when you are successful 100% of the time, your training should advance quickly. Once the dog is rapidly grabbing the dumbbell at short distances, you may slowly begin the transition to the ground a few inches at a time. Eventually you will place the dumbbell on the ground in front of the dog's feet with your hand off the dumbbell. You can test the dog's response to the retrieve command without giving a correction by keeping your hand close to the dog's head but not giving a correction unless she refuses to retrieve. If the dog gets into the habit of refusing to retrieve when no hand contact is used, do three retrieves in succession using automatic force, then apply no force on the fourth retrieve. You must give exuberant praise when the dog is performing correctly. *The praise must more than compensate for the amount of force applied.*

When the dog can retrieve the dumbbell from the ground without hesitation, you may need some assistance for the next step as the distance and distractions increase. I hook a flexi lead to the buckle collar. The dog also wears a prong collar, with a six foot lead, which my assistant holds. I throw or place the dumbbell about three feet from the dog. I keep the dog on a fairly tight lead as I give the command to fetch. I keep some pressure on the lead while my assistant uses the ear pinch, if that was the method used. If the collar twist method was used, the assistant gives a rapid jerk on the prong collar out to the dumbbell. The dog must pull against my pressure to get to the dumbbell while my assistant applies the force.

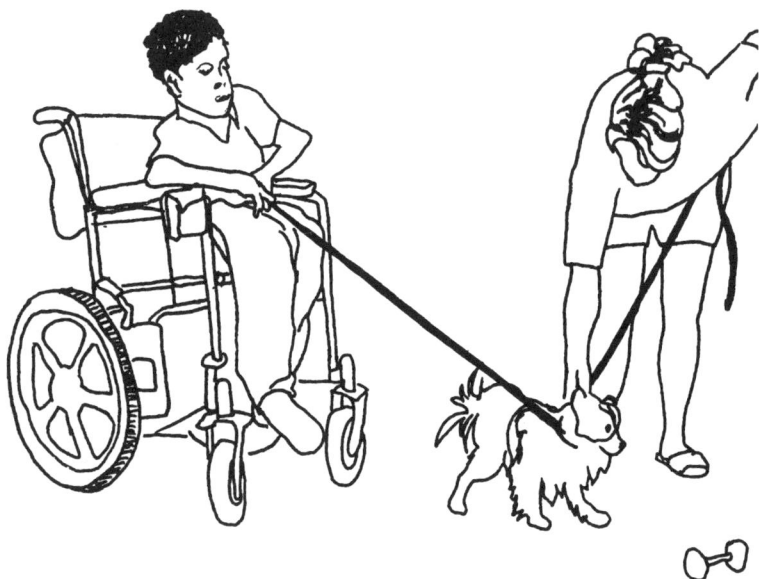

After no more than three of these corrections the dog should be flying out to the dumbbell while ignoring a fair amount of tension on my lead. I find this technique useful in that when my assistant is not available, and my dog slows up on an occasional retrieve, I can effect a correction myself by tightening up on my lead. The dog should immediately counteract the tension and dive for the dumbbell. You should train around noise, animal distractions, and with food on the ground. The dumbbell can be placed on it's end, in a corner, under a chair, or even with someone lightly standing on one end of the bell. This is the kind of reliability one should expect from this type of training method. The dog should execute the retrieve on the first command rapidly, efficiently and without hesitation.

The delivery of the dumbbell is very important and depends both on the height of your dog and your own range of motion. If you are able to reach down to take the dumbbell from a small dog, or if you are able to reach forward to take the dumbbell from a large dog that is sitting squarely in front of you, you are at a definite advantage to someone like myself who has limited reach. If I am training a large dog who presents the dumbbell from a sit in front, the dog must learn to reach forward without breaking the front to present the dumbbell within my reach. I teach the delivery separately from the retrieve.

With the dog on a prong collar and holding the dumbbell in the proper front position, I gather up the lead in the hand which will receive the dumbbell. I hold a small piece of food in between the fingers of the same hand and pull the dog's head toward my hand while letting her sniff the food. If she drops the dumbbell to get the food, she gets a retrieve correction. Her head must follow the food in my hand without getting up until I am easily able to reach the dumbbell. I exchange the food for the dumbbell when giving the release command, without allowing the dog to spit out the dumbbell prematurely or move out of the "front" position. The dog is encouraged with the aid of a food motivator and with guidance from the lead to stretch her neck forward to accommodate my reach. I once trained a Golden Retriever for a thirteen year old girl who had no reach. The dog learned to place the article in the girl's lap and pin the article with her head until the youngster could grasp it. The dog quickly learned to accommodate her owner's reach and loved being able to

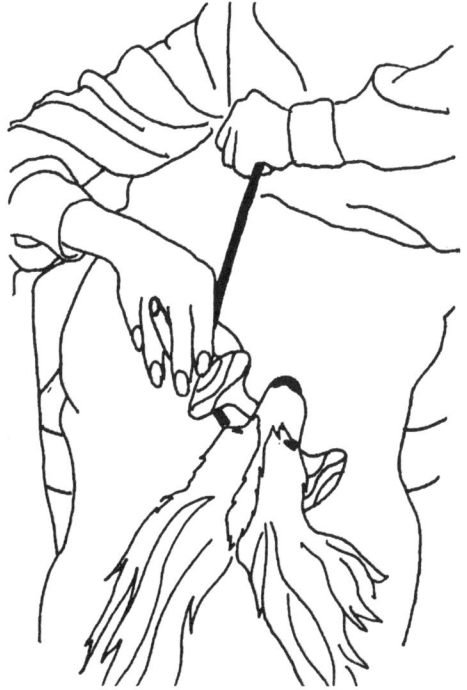

perform a well appreciated useful task for her friend. This dog learned to present everything from a TV remote to an envelope, and I have always experienced the same results from my own dogs.

Training a toy dog to reach up to present an object requires a bit more training, but the results are well worth the effort. Dogs enjoy performing useful tasks. After a bit of training, the dogs figure out by themselves the best way to present each new object retrieved.

In competition, a toy dog must retrieve the dumbbell and sit in front. I am unable to reach down to the dog's level and accept the dumbbell. The AKC regulations regarding handicapped handlers are as follows:

Section 14. Disabled Handlers. Judges may modify the specific requirements of these Regulations for handlers to the extent necessary to permit disabled handlers to compete, provided such handlers can move about the ring without physical assistance or guidance from another person, except that, subject to the Judge's instructions, anyone may position a blind handler before, between and after each exercise.

Dogs handled by such handlers shall be required to perform all parts of all exercises as described in these Regulations, and shall be penalized for failure to perform any part of an exercise.

According to the rule book, the dog must perform the retrieve and come to front as in the recall without touching the handler and within his reach. It is at this point that the dog is allowed to reach up to the handler, present the dumbbell, and without further command return to a square sit in front. This is far more work than the average dog has to perform, yet I have had a few judges penalize me for my dog jumping up on my knee to present the dumbbell. My dogs are not circus dogs who can balance their weight on their hind quarters while reaching up with an object in their mouth, and they should not be required to do so. I must also train the dog to immediately return to a square sit in front upon releasing the dumbbell without a command, because I'll get penalized for a crooked second sit even though other dogs are only judged on one sit. There are still judges out there that are unsure of how to judge a disabled handler and don't allow for the adjustments required for each disability. Only through education can judges be made aware that obedience is a sport of teamwork between dogs and handlers of all abilities, and penalties should not be given as long as the dog performs within the guidelines.

Teaching the small dog to present the dumbbell is begun with the dog on a short lead and prong collar sitting in the proper, square front position. At this point the dog is not holding the dumbbell. We are going to teach her that upon hearing her name she is going to rise up and place her front feet on your legs, balancing her weight so you can reach her muzzle. Holding a piece of food and the gathered up lead in the fingers of the hand you are going to use to take the dumbbell, say the dog's name and pull her up toward you. Gather up the slack as she comes up to your knees. When she is up on you, within reach, give her a piece of food. If you cannot pull her up while gathering up the slack, run the lead through your hand and up to your helper who is standing behind you. When you call the dog's name the helper can pull up on the lead while you guide the dog's muzzle to your hand. You will either have to mark the lead or give a signal to your helper so she will know when to stop pulling. It is difficult for your assistant to tell

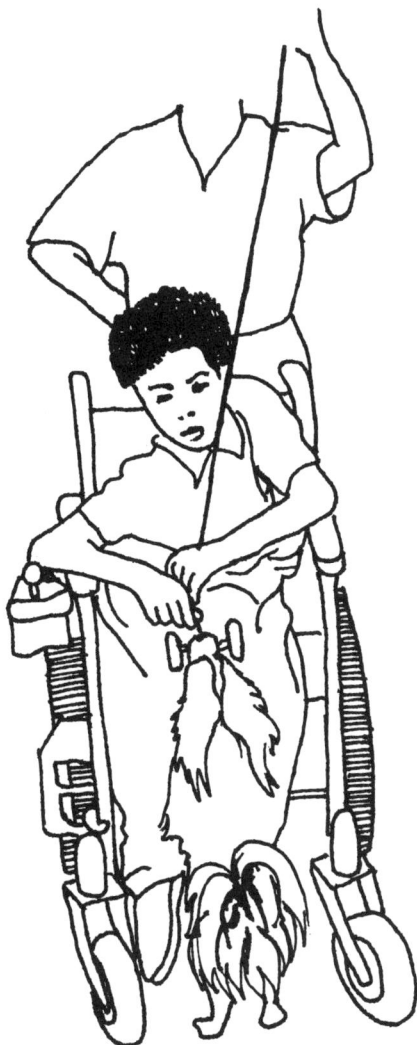

from behind when the dog is in the proper position. I've had a few helpers pull the dog so far up that she was on her tip toes or even off the ground before the helper realized she had gone too far. I use a nod of my head to signal my helper when to stop pulling, and I give the dog the food reward while drawing her into my hand, giving lots of verbal praise. The object of this lesson is to get the dog to rise up to your hand upon hearing her name. Eliminate the need for a helper before you progress to the next step.

When the dog is able to rise up out of a sit in front to receive the food, you can teach the dog to accept your touching of her head, face and muzzle before taking the food. When she rises up to your knee level, hold her in place with the lead while you touch her with the hand holding the food. In the beginning she can even nibble the food while you are touching her. Then make her wait for the food until after you have touched her. This exercise will allow you to enforce the hold while she is balancing her weight on your leg. Once the dog has learned to comfortably balance her weight on your legs while you touch her, you may introduce the return to front. After the dog accepts the food give the "Sit" command, and gently touch the dog's belly with your toe to force her to get off of you. As she settles into the sit, only give the lead enough slack so that she can slide down your leg into a straight sit without swinging off center. If you are unable to use your toe, a dowel placed under her belly or chest may help.

Dogs are able to learn sequences in putting an exercise together. The steps are as follows:

1.   A lead pull up on the prong using the dog's name.

2.   A food reward and verbal praise when the dog rises.

3.   A sit command using a gentle foot correction and a taut lead that guides into a straight sit.

4.   Verbal praise when the dog is sitting.

Presenting the Dumbbell

To teach the dog to present the dumbbell, I begin with the dog reaching up to my lap. I give the fetch command and place the dumbbell in the dog's mouth. I praise the dog for holding the dumbbell within my reach and gently scratch the dog's face and head. I then give the command "Out," take the dumbbell and give the command "Sit."   I do not keep the dog standing for excessive periods of time on her rear legs.

This position is not natural for a dog, and her hindquarters must be conditioned slowly to comfortably accept this stance. A young, physically immature dog can be taught the retrieve but the presentation should be taught from a bed or chair so as not to put undue strain on the rear legs.

While the dog is learning to hold the dumbbell within reach of your hand, she is also learning the correct position to facilitate your taking the dumbbell from her. For example, I always use my right hand to take the dumbbell, and I always take it from the dog's left side of the mouth. When the dog is facing me her left side is closest to my right hand. The dog must learn, in my case, to present objects towards my right hand. When the dog learns this concept by repeatedly releasing the dumbbell to my right hand, I then reinforce the lesson by placing most of the bar of the dumbbell towards the opposite side of the dog's mouth. When I try to take the dumbbell the dog realizes I cannot reach it. Some dogs instinctively adjust the dumbbell to accommodate me. Others need a slight tap on the far end of the dumbbell to slide the bell in the mouth so it protrudes out the correct side. A correctly trained dog should be able to retrieve a variety of dumb-

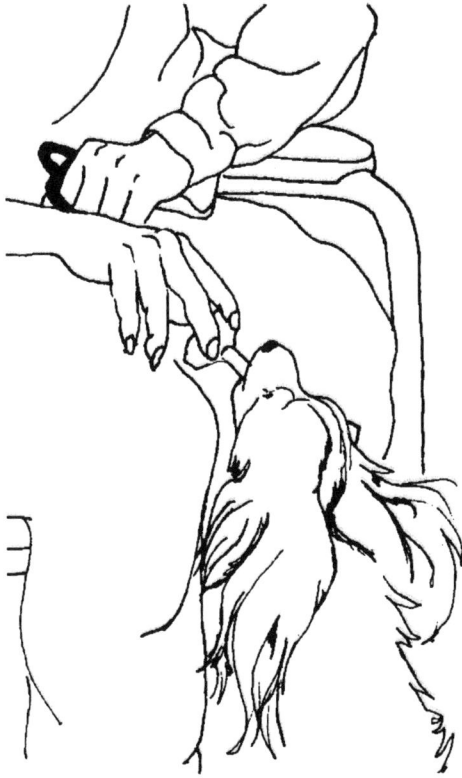

bells. The end piece should not obscure the dog's vision and it should not be too heavy to carry it over the jump. It is more important that the dumbbell should be easy for the handler to grasp. I cannot adequately describe the feelings between dog and handler when the dog realizes her accomplishment of fulfilling a need for her handler. When the dog understands that you can only grasp an object from her in a certain way, she will learn to adjust anything she brings to you. This is the essence of dog training and I believe it can be accomplished with great satisfaction by people with limited physical ability.

The final step in the presentation is to get the dog to reach up to deliver the dumbbell and this is where your foundation of the forced retrieve will benefit you. If a dog has been properly taught to retrieve and hold a dumbbell, she will easily reach up upon command to effect the delivery. If she inadvertently drops the dumb-bell on her way up to your lap, a quick, efficient correction can be given by you or your helper to remind the dog that she must never drop the dumbbell. The dog will learn to focus on the retrieve of the dumbbell and she will concentrate on the delivery to your hand, thereby ignoring any and all distractions that might occur during the exercise. The retrieve work should carry over into all of your other exercises, reinforcing your dog's concentration on you.

Once the dog is reliably retrieving from a short distance and is delivering the dumbbell to hand, you can teach longer retrieves while incorporating a "blind" retrieve. A blind retrieve is one in which the dog must fetch an object that she can not see. Sometimes a dumbbell can become hidden in the grass, but a well-trained dog should make a reasonable search. This exercise increases the reliability of the directed retrieve and enables one to teach go-outs with the aid of a hidden dowel.

Begin with increasing the distance of the retrieve within the dog's sight. Leave the dog on a sit stay and place the dumbbell ten feet away, directly in front of the dog. Upon returning to the dog, send her for the dumbbell. If the dog executes a satisfactory retrieve, you may gradually increase the distance to the point that the dog is proficient at sixty foot retrieves. Always place the dumbbell in a perfectly straight line from the dog, so she learns to expect the dumbbell will always be in front of her. When the dog is satisfactorily performing sixty foot retrieves in different locations under varying distractions, shorten up the retrieve to six feet. Leave the dog on a sit stay, but this time place the dumbbell with your back to the dog so she doesn't see the dumbbell placed. As with all retrieves, if your dog refuses or hesitates you always have the force retrieve correction to fall back on. Gradually increase the distance of the blind retrieve to sixty feet as the dog gains confidence. You may also increase the difficulty by using locations with tall grass, placing the dumbbell in a hole, or partially hiding it under a mat. Your dog must learn that when she is sent to retrieve the dumbbell it is always straight ahead of her and that she must never return without it. You now have the foundation for the more advanced exercises.

Training the Useful Retrieve

Since you have devoted so much time and effort to teaching your dog to retrieve a dumbbell, why not spend a couple of extra hours teaching her to retrieve useful objects for you? Once you have laid the necessary foundation for the retrieve, you simply need to introduce objects of varying shape, texture and weight. It is important in the beginning stages to not discourage the dog by using objects that she simply can not pick up, or by overwhelming her with too many things before she is ready.

Let's begin with a pencil. It is similar to a dumbbell, but is thinner, lighter, longer and will lie flat on the ground Sit the dog on the bed and have her hold the pencil in her mouth. You may say, "Fetch the pencil", thereby teaching the dog the names of objects for future reference. The dog must hold each object cleanly, efficiently and without rolling or mouthing as she was taught with the dumbbell. But, the dog does not ever have to sit front upon the delivery or be quite as fast or accurate on the pick up. Later on when she is asked to retrieve new and complicated objects, the dog will have to think about how best to accomplish this task. The dog will not hesitate on the now familiar dumbbell, but she may stop for a moment to figure out the new article until becoming more proficient in the retrieving exercise.

When the dog is correctly holding the pencil in the center, you may place the pencil on the bed and guide the dog to pick it up by using either the collar or the ear method. Do not give in to the dog if she seems to have difficulty picking up the pencil lying flat on the bed. She will figure it out if you consistently use your original method of training the retrieve. Once the dog is consistently retrieving the pencil, have her take it from you while she is reaching up to you, using the same method as with the dumbbell. Show her through constant repetition how best to hold and present the pencil to you, because she has no end pieces to guide her. Be patient, and remember to praise the dog for her efforts. Place or throw the pencil on the floor commanding "Fetch the pencil", and always be consistent in the manner in which you take it from her mouth. When the dog is doing well at retrieving a pencil, try a metal or plastic pen using the same technique.

The next progression is to have the dog retrieve her leash. I fold the leash and place it in the dog's mouth. Every time I introduce a new object when teaching the useful retrieve, I place the object properly in the dog's mouth to accustom her to the feel of the object and to the correct way it is to be held. Only when the dog is competently holding the new article do you progress to the retrieve on the bed. This is where you are in control and must effect a swift, decisive correction. When this part of the training is accomplished, you place the object in the dog's mouth while she is reaching up to you. At this time, you are teaching the dog how to properly present each new article to you. Every article may be given a name. Some dogs will have more difficulty with different objects depending on the object's shape, the dog's muzzle configuration, and your ability to grasp the object. At this point you and your dog should be working as a team, and with a fair amount of patience and tolerance you can work out each new challenge as it presents itself.

I usually progress to the following objects:

An envelope -- you may slightly bend the envelope until the dog gets used to picking it up when it is lying flat.

A glove -- as with all objects, do not allow mouthing, rolling, tossing or chewing.

A spoon -- some dogs do not like the taste of metal, so spend extra time getting the dog used to the feel of it in her mouth. If you have a significant battle over metal, have the dog's teeth checked by your vet or canine dentist. Some dogs, especially toy breeds, experience tooth or gum disease which should be attended to before continuing this phase of training.

A small box -- Size and weight should always be consistent with the size of the dog.

A makeup case -- You can slowly add objects to the case.

A key ring with keys -- I find this to be difficult for some dogs and I usually leave it for last, then I add one key at a time.

Larger dogs can be trained to pick up their food dishes, bring in the newspaper, carry a handbag or groceries, or find the TV remote control.

Once you have mastered these simple, day-to-day objects, you can give the dog the opportunity to be a true working companion. If the dog loves you, she will enjoy pleasing you. If you communicate to the dog how much her efforts please you, she will begin to anticipate your needs and will recognize your dependency on her assistance. The dog will appreciate and enjoy her role as your helper, and she will gain a useful importance to her life. Throughout the centuries of human/dog relationships, dogs have worked for their owners. Livestock dogs work sheep or cattle, retrievers hunt and retrieve game, northern breeds pull sleds, and many dogs are bred to guard their family or property. These dogs use their innate natural ability. The difference in training the retrieve is that it can be accomplished regardless of the dog's natural ability or the handler's disability.

The dogs and I do demonstrations for schools, nursing homes and various other public organizations. I believe it is my duty as a breeder/ trainer/ exhibitor to promote dogs as useful members of our society especially in this day of much negative dog publicity. We do some heeling, recalls, jumping, retrieving all tailored to the audience of the day. I encourage participation and I solicit people to help out with the dog's performance. We usually end on a "trick" that I teach my advanced dogs who are trained to retrieve only for me. I begin by asking a person for a dollar bill. The person hesitantly pulls out a dollar where upon I ask them to throw it on the floor. They reluctantly toss the bill down and my dog upon command promptly retrieves and delivers the dollar to me. I pocket the bill and ask for a ten dollar bill. The audience laughs and I explain that my dogs really earn their keep. I once fleeced one hundred dollars from a man before he caught on to my game. Yes -- I did return the bills, all the while thinking, " a fool and his money....."

Chapter Twelve

TEACHING JUMPING

Before teaching a dog to jump she must be physically mature. Her joints and ligaments must be fully developed in order to handle the stress of jumping. She must also be in fit condition and must not be overweight. If the dog is not in good athletic shape you must condition her with a proper diet and moderate exercise over a period of time. The dog must also be free of genetic defects such as hip dysplasia or patella luxation.

Since I cannot leap over the jump with the dog, my method of teaching a dog to jump differs from most. I use a very loose lead on a buckle collar, or a choke collar on the dead ring, so I do not pull the dog off stride as she jumps. The first obstacle I use is a broad jump turned on end, and I run by the jump with the dog by my left side. I do not give a heel command as I start, I just want the dog moving alongside my chair. I want her to concentrate on the jump, not on me, so she learns to gauge her stride for the take off and landing. I move the dog forward in a trot and speed up slightly as I approach the jump. As the dog begins to jump I give the command "Hup," and when all four feet have landed on the other side I continue forward in a straight line for a couple of steps while praising the dog. Then I release the dog and give exuberant praise. I repeat this about

five times and then quit, before the dog gets tired or bored. I use this exercise in between teaching other less stimulating exercises or before heeling, as it elevates the dog's mood for the training session. My concern, at this point, is not to gain height on the jump but to familiarize the dog with the command and the act of concentrating on the jump. I use a variety of obstacles without sides in the beginning, such as a rolled up mat or an over-turned lawn chair, depending upon the size of the dog. The dog enjoys leaping over things as long as the height is comfortable and you do not repeat the exercise to the point of exhaustion or boredom. It is very important to keep the dog on a loose lead and not put pressure on her neck, thereby pulling her off balance. Once a dog is confident in her ability to jump, you may increase the height slowly by an inch or two at a time. When I introduce the high jump, I use a jump with low sides so my lead doesn't get hung up as I go by. You must not interrupt the fluidity of the dog's movement with inept lead handling, and you must never ask a dog to jump a hurdle that she is unable to manage. The most difficult concept for the dog is when the jump height is even with or exceeds her eye level. At this point, a dog may elect to go around the jump rather than leap over something when she cannot see her landing point. You can begin proofing the dog at much lower heights by tempting her to come around the jump with food or distractions but not allowing her to do so with a lead correction back over the jump. As soon as the dog is committed to the jump, you must remember to keep the lead loose.

In the final stages of perfecting the broad jump, a person in a wheelchair must position herself the required two foot distance from the jump while allowing enough room for the dog to finish once the handler has made the pivot. Since the pivot is not always executed as smoothly in a wheelchair as by someone standing, the dog must be well conditioned to jump straight down the center of the jump and to not focus on your movements as you turn. To get the dog to focus straight ahead, I use a dumbbell placed in the center line of the jump in a spot where the dog can comfortably land before retrieving and then pivoting front. When the

dog automatically begins to focus down the center, I alternate between placing the dumbbell and tossing it while the dog is jumping. I also have a helper place the dumbbell when the dog is not watching. I will then substitute a small dowel for the dumbbell so the dog is never certain whether it is a retrieve or merely a jump. In teaching the broad jump, I frequently jump the dog in the opposite direction. This will give the dog the lift without changing the perception of the jump from the dog's point of view. I also place short dowels on both sides of the jump with thin string connecting them across the top. The dog won't see the string but her feet will hit it if she doesn't clear the jump properly.

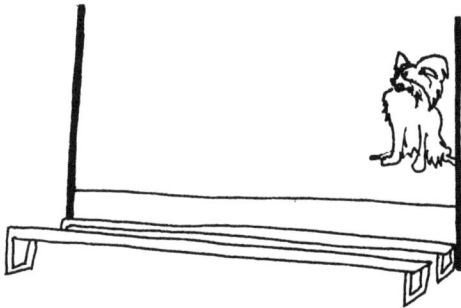

In the retrieve over the high jump, a wheelchair user must make modifications that are allowable according to the AKC rules and guidelines. My personal belief is that a person who wheels up to the jump and tosses the dumbbell over aides the dog and might cause some prejudice in a competitive class. I prefer to go around the jump when placing the dumbbell because it tempts the dog to go around, plus she must maintain a longer sit stay while awaiting your return. This method

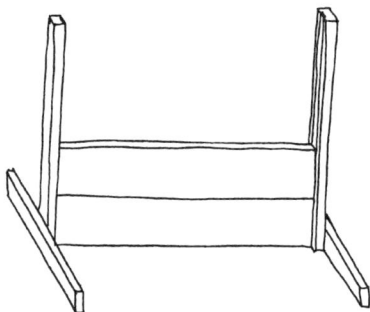

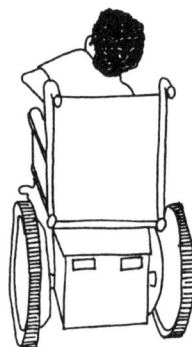

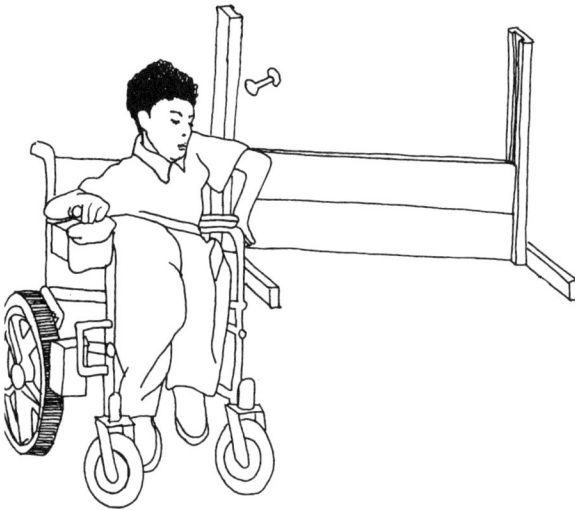

takes a bit more training on the part of the handicapped handler, but it is far more impressive to the judges and spectators. The extra effort makes for a steadier and more reliable dog. The training of a dog by a handicapped handler is far more intricate and painstaking than that done by most able-bodied handlers. These efforts should be appreciated by judges and fellow exhibitors, even in extremely competitive situations.

I used to train with a friend, who had sporting dogs, that came from breeders specializing in field dogs with strong hunting instincts. My friend was very adept at being my helper. She followed my instructions making carefully timed corrections when I was unable to physically reach my dogs. Because of the teamwork we developed over years of training together, I was able to obtain many obedience titles during the time we worked together. We trained in numerous locations in preparation for the various distractions encountered at obedience trials. My dogs were trustworthy off lead. I could release them between exercises knowing they would come when called. My friend, though a dedicated trainer, was unwilling to take the painstaking training time and effort needed to override the intense flight drive instinctively bred into her dogs. Every training session was interrupted by hunting for one of her dogs who managed to escape during an off lead exercise.

At one training session one of her dogs cleared the high jump but bypassed the dumbbell. He continued going until he found a pony grazing in a field. Chasing the pony was a lot more fun than training that day. Another occasion found him running down the median strip of a busy highway, following a car with balloons hanging out the windows.

Fortunately, he was never killed or seriously injured in his escapades but it certainly took the pleasure out of training. I quickly learned to work my dogs first and put them back in the van when finished because I never knew how my friend's training session would end. Due to her hard work and perserverence she managed to get several Utility titles on her dogs. However, the patches of gray I sport on my head are the results of my acquaintences with a Springer and a couple of Brittanys.

Chapter Thirteen

ADVANCED TRAINING

Most of the training for Utility is the same for all handlers, regardless of their physical abilities. The foundation of the utility exercises goes back to the basics of trust and consistency between dog and handler. The signal exercises must be physically comfortable for the handler and visible to the dog. Signals should be introduced in the early stages of training, and the judge should be alerted to any modifications before the start of the exercise.

Scent Discrimination -- The Articles

There are many ways to teach the scent portion of the articles. The basic difference with a physically challenged trainer is the need to work with the dog at the same level of the handler's reach.

The dog should already be accustomed to properly holding and retrieving both metal and leather articles as taught in the retrieving section of this book. I always begin teaching scent with a metal article. You can feel the difference in temperature between a cold unscented article and one which has been vigorously rubbed. This is an advantage to the dog. I think the dog can discriminate scent easier on metal because leather has an overriding scent of its own. Most dogs find leather more enjoyable to pick up so I leave it for last. If the dog is successful with the metal article she gets the reward of ending the exercise on the leather. If she does not do the metal correctly she is worked until she is successful.

I use a round metal macramé hoop to which I attach the articles using metal curtain rings. These

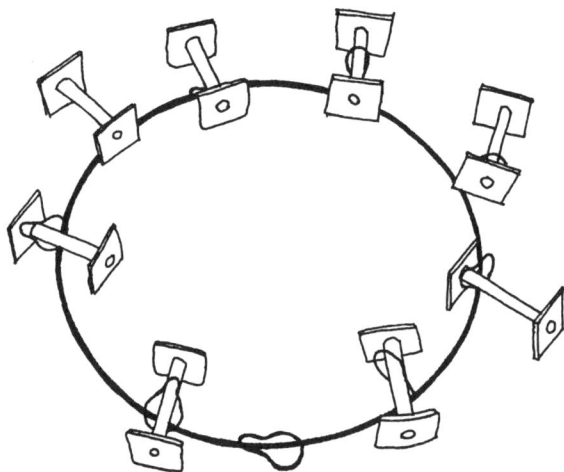

hoops can be purchased at craft shops. They come in several sizes, are easily carried and hold little scent of their own when handled lightly. Another advantage is that you can easily add articles to them with the metal curtain hooks. The hooks can be purchased at linen or hardware stores.

I begin with one metal article attached to the hoop. I start training the toy dogs on a card table and the large dogs on the bed. I place the dog on a down about two inches from the unscented articles on the ring. While the dog is on a down stay I let her watch as I vigorously rub the bar of the metal article. I only use single bar articles because they take less time to scent and they allow a neater retrieve. They are also lighter in weight. I scent the article for about one minute. If it is a particularly cold day I have difficulty imparting scent on the articles. I spray a fine mist of water on my hands and I find it easier for the dog to pick up my scent. I often lightly wet my hands on a cold dry day before entering the Utility ring. When I think the article is sufficiently scented I hold it up to the dog's nose asking her to "Sniff it". I then place it one inch away from the unscented article. I give the command, "Find it". The dog can just stretch her head to get the article. It doesn't matter whether or not she gets up to get it. If she needs motivation I gently tug the dog forward on the lead. If she picks up the correct article I praise her exuberantly. I then gently take the article, being careful not to hit it against her teeth. If she rolls or drops it, I correct as I described in the force retrieve. I do not let any bad habits form at this beginning stage.

If she selects the wrong article the curtain hook prevents the dog from picking it up. I give the dog the chance to figure it out. If she finds the correct one I praise as I previously described. If she persists in picking up the wrong one, I put the scented article up to her nose and then reposition it on the ring. I continue this progression until she chooses the correct article. If the dog refuses to pick up the article, I remove the ring with the article attached leaving the correct article down. I force her on the scented article. Only when she is retrieving the article by itself do I continue working with the ring.

When the dog selects the correct article I repeat the exercise with a new freshly scented metal article positioning it on the other side of the unscented one. Depending upon how the dog progresses I proceed as previously described. The next time I place the scented article one inch behind the unscented one. If she appears to be scenting the correct article I add another unscented metal article to the ring and work with one final freshly scented article. I only work metal articles at this stage.

The key to success with this method is working the dog close to the articles so she doesn't confuse it with the forced retrieve where she is required to run out and bring any object back. I use a fresh, scented article each time so she doesn't have the aid of the scent of her own saliva. I place the articles one or two inches apart so the dog can easily catch the scent. I do this in an area free of strong air currents so the scent doesn't blow onto the unscented article.

When I think the dog has grasped the concept of scenting, I send her several feet from the ring of articles. If she makes a mistake, I pick up the scented article, let her sniff it , and then replace it. I rotate the articles on the ring but by placing them around the ring the dog learns to work in a circle. When I have four unscented articles down, I may occasionally put the scented one in the center.

The next step is to sit the dog about four feet from the ring. I place the article and return to the dog. I pivot her in a full, tight circle returning to a sit in the original position facing the ring. This prevents the dog from remembering where I placed the article. She should use her nose now if before she was depending on sight. If the dog learns to pick up the only article without the curtain hook, I put a hook on the scented one also. This should not matter to a force retrieve trained dog. I gradually increase the distance between the dog and the ring. When the dog consistently responds correctly, I face the dog away from the ring, place the article, return to the dog, pivot, sit, and send.

At this stage of training I work with distractions and only scent the article for 30 seconds. I have other people lightly scent the "wrong" articles. I work on grass, dirt, or carpet. If possible, I use other animals or people as distractions near the ring.

I introduce the leather articles in the same manner. When the dog is successfully working the leathers several inches away, I gradually add metals until both sets are down. When the dog is reliable with all the articles, I increase the distance at which they are placed around the ring until they are three to four inches apart. I think it is interesting that the AKC requires the articles to be placed six inches apart regardless of the size of the dog. Because toy dogs are at a disadvantage, I am not in a hurry to push them too fast at this stage. Eventually I remove the ring and place the articles six inches apart working the dog back to the AKC required 20 foot distance away from the pile. If the dog makes mistakes I return to the ring.

If a dog, who has been consistently working the articles correctly, has an off day I quit for that day. Sometime medications a dog is taking have an adverse effect on her scenting ability. I give her the benefit of the doubt when she is otherwise reliable.

Before you enter a trial, work the dog in various weather conditions. Heat, humidity, and wind all have an effect on scenting conditions. Have different people scent the "wrong" articles for you. If you encounter a problem day, do not hesitate to go back on the ring, shorten the distance you are working or place the articles closer together.

Directed Retrieve

In the directed retrieve, the dog may have to line up on the turn with a wheel or the side of the chair depending on the height or neck length of the dog. The handicapped handler is at a definite disadvantage by not being able to reach down to the dog's eye level to give a direction. Therefore, the dog must be well-schooled in taking a line and in executing a blind retrieve. Pivots, with the front wheel position straight, are critical for small dogs.

The foundation of the go-outs is the blind retrieve. I begin by having the dog retrieve a dowel. For small dogs I use a three inch long, 1/2 inch diameter wooden dowel. For large dogs I use a dowel with maximum measurements of five inches long, one inch diameter. This method is successful only with dogs that are properly force retrieved as earlier described in the chapter on retrieving.

I begin training in a long hallway or on a long narrow sidewalk. I place the dowel three feet in front of the dog who is on a sit stay. After returning to the dog I command, "Go fetch." Upon a successful retrieve, I give exuberant praise. On the next retrieve I place three dowels, each a foot further away from the dog. When the dog completes the first

retrieve, I have her finish. I then send her for the second dowel. If the dog hesitates or refuses she gets a retrieve correction. After going to heel, she is sent for the third dowel. It doesn't matter which dowel is retrieved as long as the dog continues to go out on the first command. I gradually work the dog back to a distance of at least sixty feet with dowels placed a foot or two behind each other. The dog is to learn the concept that if she continues to go out in a straight line there will always be something out there to retrieve. At this stage you can just use the command, "go." You may make the dowels less visible by partially covering them with grass or a piece of cloth. The dog should be excited to run out for a long distance retrieve. I hype the dog up by saying, "Ready, are you ready, ready?" in an excited tone just prior to giving the "go" command. This cues the dog into knowing it is a long straight go-out. In the ring the judge usually asks if you are ready. I always nod my head or say "Yes." But before the go-outs I reply with a firm "Ready" which cues the dog into the go-out instead of a glove retrieve.

At this point you can work in a ring between the jumps. I begin with two dowels which are placed one on each side of the middle ring stanchion. I work the dog three feet from the dowels gradually moving back until the dog retrieves the length of the ring through the jumps and sometimes out the ring.

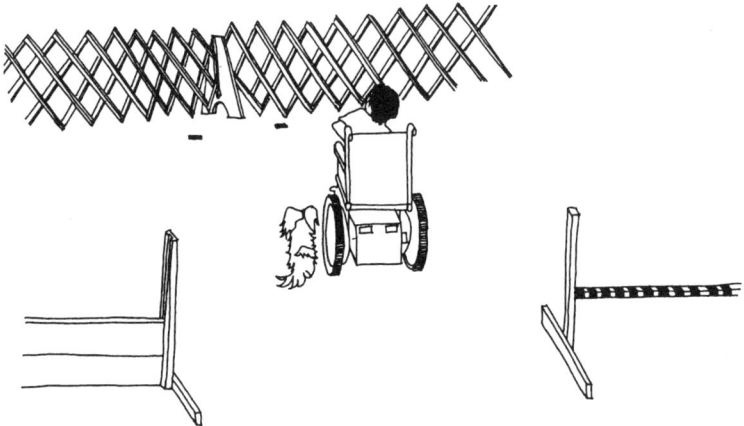

When the dog is totally reliable, I place gloves at the corners but I insist that on the "Ready, go," only the dowel is retrieved.

The turn and sit is introduced three feet from the dowels. The dog is placed on a stand facing the dowels. I am directly behind the dog holding the lead. I say the dog's name, "Suki" and as the dog turns around I give the sit command. If the dog doesn't turn, I help her with a tug on the lead. If she doesn't sit immediately or creeps forward, I move in and enforce the sit.

I reward the sit with food. Then I give the "Fetch" command and I expect the dog to turn and retrieve the dowels. I give enthusiastic praise for the retrieve. I work further back from the dog until she reliably turns and sits from a stand facing the dowels from three feet away. I never move back if the dog creeps a foot or more toward me. I use my chair to block the forward movement. As I move back to the opposite end of the ring, I intermittently reward the sit with food or alternate with the "Fetch." Soon I am able to bring the dog back, send her on "Go," and command "Sit" before she reaches the dowel. With some highly retrieve motivated dogs, I keep them on a line for awhile so I can halt them on my sit command. Sometimes I go out and give a piece of hot dog for the sit and sometimes I say "Fetch" and insist on a retrieve down the middle of the ring. If the dog doesn't sit I follow the dog out as quietly as I can and enforce the sit before she retrieves the dowel. If the dog hears me, I have a helper sneak up on her and enforce the sit. Once the dog is reliable, I alternate between turn and sits and the retrieve.

If I say, "Go" and then,"Sit," I go out with a food reward. I then bring the dog back down the middle between the jumps. The next command will be "Go" and as the dog approaches the dowel I'll say "Fetch." If the dog should ever begin to anticipate the turn and sit or begin to shorten up on the "go-out," I always have the dowel retrieve to reinforce the command. I or a helper occasionally put several gloves out along the back of the ring as a way of proofing the dog against going out to the corners. I work the jumps separately until the go-outs are perfect and the dog never considers going out over the jumps.

Because of my limited arm reach and extension, I use food in my hand to teach the dog to focus on the specific jumps. I always keep the jumps close together until the dog consistently watches my hand movements for directed jumping. Gradually I increase the distance between the jumps. I work the dog at all angles from the jumps and I only combine the go-outs when the dog can take direction. At this stage, I have several options for ending the exercise. I can reward the turn and sit. I can reward the correct jump after the turn and sit, or I can give the fetch either down and back thru the middle or back over a jump and give food and praise.

I continue to cue the dog with "Ready." After executing the moving stand I hurry to the spot where the judge will issue the directed jumping. I will quietly say "Ready" to the dog before the judge has a chance to speak. I often use the opportunity to cue the dog while the judge is marking my moving stand score. I don't wait for the judge to move me to the directed jumping exercise. I instead try to beat him to the spot. It makes me look rather efficient when I am in fact using the time to get my dog focused on the long straight go-out.

After obtaining my American UD on my Golden Retriever, "Chico" I began losing volume in my voice. I never had a very loud voice due to respiratory problems but about that time my voice was barely above a whisper. Chico was a very high energy dog used to my old voice. He was willing to work for me especially if he could have fun at the same time. When I taught blind retrieves I made them quite long because I used to do a little field work with him. I used those blind retrieves as a basis for my go-outs.

I decided to try for his Canadian UD and in preparation I attended an outdoor match. The rings had ropes instead of ring gates and I have a bit of a depth perception problem. That day I sent Chico on the first go-out and realized he had just passed under the rope. I tried to command "Chico, sit" but he never heard me. He kept going in a straight line, much to the amazement of not only my judge but the judge in the next ring through which he raced. He continued until he came upon an unsuspecting couple having lunch up on the hill a quarter of a mile away. Chico, thinking their lunch bag was his target, snatched it up, pivoted around, and raced back through the rings depositing the bag in my lap. I said to the amazed judge, "Guess he didn't hear the 'Sit'."

Chapter Fourteen

HAPPY TALES

All of my training methods take extreme patience and consideration for the dog in the teaching process. Obedience titles are not easily earned by any handler. Training by disabled handlers presents even more of a challenge. My enjoyment of dog training more than compensates for my efforts. Success in obedience competition further enhances the experience. I began training dogs 25 years ago when a Collie I received as a gift ate my mother's kitchen. Handicapped handlers were new to the sport of obedience at that time, and we were not exactly welcomed. Judges had to change their perception of the ideal performance by a handler on two feet to one with wheels and very limited muscular ability.

My dogs' love of the work and their obvious devotion to me has helped convert judges, exhibitors, spectators and the American Kennel Club to the acceptance of handicapped handlers in the sport. Because of my involvement with showing dogs, the general public has had more exposure to the physically disabled. I would like to think that my dogs and I have helped change a few minds about what handicapped people can accomplish. The dogs have certainly contributed to my longevity. My Chesapeake Bay Retriever, "Cloudy," started me in the sport and earned my first CDX, TD, WC, and Can. CD. I then trained my wonderful Golden Retriever, "Chico" to a UDT, WC., and Can CDX. I have had three CH, UDT Papillons, one of which was the breed's first CH. UDT bitch who went onto become a Dam of Merit. I've earned six tracking titles, six UD's and I've finished several breed Champions. I've bred many breed and obedience titled Papillons under the Kine-ahora prefix. Now I am venturing into the sport of agility. Most satisfying are the wonderful dogs with whom I have worked, the many friendships I have made and the difference I hope I have made in the sport of showing dogs. If you truly love and appreciate your dog's devotion and working ability, obedience competition is a sport that can be enjoyed by anyone, regardless of his or her physical strength. At the very least, you will end up with a companion, without equal, that will give many years of service, devotion and companionship.